PRACTISING RESURRECTION

This is a book that comprehensively blows apart just why the followers of Jesus cannot be ordinary or satisfied with the way things are. Cris challenges us to live lives utterly riddled with the resurrection of Christ . . . read it and you will see that it all makes sense.

Jill Rowe
Oasis Ethos Development and Resourcing Director

Cris is a good guy who loves Jesus and practices what he preaches and I promise you his book will get you noticed. It will have you practising resurrection in your home, street and town centre. Escape the monotony of being a safe, hidden Saturday Christian. Trust that the madness of Easter Sunday is still happening.

Andy Flannagan, Director
Christian Socialist Movement

Cris is a man of real integrity, someone whose passion is clearly evident not only in his words but in the way he lives his life. This book shares that passion to help us see past the trappings of religion and get back to knowing Jesus, his power and his presence in our lives. It reawakens hope for our world, gives us a gracious kick on the behind and challenges us to be a part of the change we long to see.

Mike Pilavachi
Soul Survivor Ministries

This is a book for those who want to see more clearly. To have their eyes opened to see the real Jesus and follow Him in the great adventure of living the resurrection life. Cris has drawn on his relationship with God, experience of following Him and some deep thinking to give us a passionate, honest and intelligent vision of the life of a disciple and the call for the transformation of society.

David Westlake
Tearfund

Many people talk about a more authentic church from the comfort of their office but having worked with Cris I can say that he doesn't just talk the talk, he walks the walk. Cris has written a manifesto for the 'new Victorians,' an integrated lifestyle that expresses the transformative nature of the resurrection of Jesus Christ. I commend this book to you, not just because of its excellent content, but because of the integrity of the voice behind it.

Rev'd Will Van Der Hart
Vicar St Peter's West Harrow

I've known Cris for quite a few years now – I'm proud to call him a friend. Cris is a thinker, a doer and a lover of Jesus. He's not one of those people who accepts the status-quo or moans about it from the sidelines. My hope as you read this book is that some of Cris's love for Jesus and the mission of his followers will rub off on you – as it has on me – and that you'll embrace everything God is calling you to do in living that love out.

Wendy Beech-Ward
Director of Spring Harvest

PRACTISING RESURRECTION:

the church being Jesus' hands, feet and heart

Cris Rogers

Authentic

First published 2010 by Authentic Media Limited
Milton Keynes
www.authenticmedia.co.uk

British Library Cataloguing in Publication Data
A catalogue record for this book is available from the British Library
ISBN 978-1-85078-860-7

Cover design by fourninezero design.
Printed in Great Britain by J.F. Print, Sparkford

Contents

SHOUT-OUTS . . .

This book is dedicated to all those who still believe in Jesus' resurrection community.

Beki, my best and perfect friend. Thank you for your freedom in allowing me to process this stuff and then spend hours writing it down, and then you having to read it. Thanks for letting me go half way around the world to research and learn, and thank you for allowing me grace when I don't practise what I preach. This is for you.

A big shout-out to my homeless friend, Jesus: thank you for giving me a kick.

We can change it for everyone
Our generation can be the sun
Love is revolution, you don't need a gun
Make it happen together as one
Cos love is just like oxygen
Don't let our people get overrun

All people, all life under the sun
Make it happen,
What do we want to become?
Beauty,
Friendship,
Justice,
Everyone,
everyone com'on

People uprise
Everyone uprise
Unite tonight
Love uprise

'England Uprise' by Nizlopi

FOREWORD

Living sacrifices

Revolution is in the air. A new generation of Christians are aware that the world we have been handed is very fragile, and that the Christian faith is not just about going up when we die but about bringing God's kingdom down.

There is a suspicion about the peace that 'Rome' offers, a counterfeit peace that is rooted in fear and retaliation, and begets the very evil it seeks to destroy. A new generation is convinced that God's dream looks different than Wall Street's dream. There is a deep conviction that a sustainable world seeks only for our daily bread rather than stockpiling stuff in barns or banks for tomorrow. And there is a winsome delight that the lilies of the field shame Solomon in all his splendour . . . or that of any royalty, for that matter. And there is a hunger for justice, for compassion, for mercy to flow through these streets of injustice.

But don't be fooled into thinking this is just a movement of youthful naivety and idealism. It seems the Spirit is up to something much more. The young are dreaming ancient dreams, but the old are seeing new visions. There are thoughtful, theologically grounded, missional Christians going into the world as doctors and lawyers, poets and artists, activists and teachers to do something about oppression, to change the patterns of this world until they conform to the norms of the upside down kingdom of God that belongs to the poor, not just the middle class, and to the peacemakers, not the war-makers, and to the meek, in this age that adores aggression.

Cris Rogers is one of those voices that are inviting us into life – real life, not one that teaches us happiness can be purchased. Cris' words will inspire you and dare you not to settle for anything short of God's dream. Cris is one more sign of a new movement of young and old committed to the radical Jesus who told the religious elite that the tax collectors and prostitutes were entering the kingdom ahead of them.

It is this non-violent Jesus of scandalous grace who loved his enemies so much he died for them on the cross. And it is this Jesus who triumphed over all death and suffering and meanness as he rose from the grave, and who made a spectacle of the cross and exposed the powers of this world. He laughed at death. He subverted power. It is that seditious resurrection which Cris calls us to practise, to enact – to live every day, every moment. May this book move us all a little closer to the revolution of God and the holy mischief of Christian trouble-makers throughout history; may it move us to live the revolution that dances, that interrupts injustice with grace, that destroys evil by loving evildoers, that laughs at fear and recessions, and trusts in the God who has overcome the world.

May God bless you with discomfort at easy answers, half-truths and superficial relationships, so that you may live deep within your heart.

May God bless you with anger at injustice, oppression and exploitation of people, so that you may work for justice, freedom and peace.

May God bless you with tears to shed for those who suffer from pain, rejection, starvation and war, so that you may reach out your hand to comfort them and to turn their pain into joy.

And may God bless you with enough foolishness to believe that you can make a difference in this world, so that you can do what others claim cannot be done.

Amen.

Shane Claiborne
author, activist, and recovering sinner
www.thesimpleway.org

0.

Hey!

Since Sinai God has been offering a covenant in which the haves and have nots are bound together.

Walter Brueggemann, The Prophetic Imagination (Philadelphia: Fortress Press, 2001), p.56.

This is where it starts

Hey, my name is Cris Rogers and I believe in the resurrection. Phew! There, I said it. Some people would see me as a religious nutter for saying that, but it is true. I believe in the resurrection, I believe a man died and came back to life, I believe it has power to restore lives, I believe it is the one event on which everything hinges . . . and this is a book about it.

As a child I was told stories of Jesus, his death and resurrection. It was just another magic story like *Rumpelstiltskin*, the seven dwarves and talking trains. Although *Thomas the Tank Engine* was good fun, it was never a story based upon reality!

The resurrection was boxed as one of those things adults talk about, but I never saw it as something that real or having real power. Jesus, Santa, the Easter Bunny and talking animals were all things I heard of but never saw in the reality of life. It was as though the resurrection existed in some magical world, but not here in the real world. By the time I hit my teens the thought of magic had gone and so had the belief in the resurrection. Life was lacking hope and meaning and I didn't really see the point to it all.

But now I believe. Not because I have read about it or been convinced because of good arguments, but because I have seen it all around me and seen that it is good!

But having said that, I need to get something off my chest, and I hope that you will humour me and keep reading. For some time now I have had this gut-wrenching feeling that something's not working, or at least not for me, and that there has to be something more than what I keep experiencing. And this thing that I am not so sure about is something that I have been involved with for quite a while now, and what's even worse is it's something that I am very committed to. This thing is religion.

Falling in love

I met Jesus and his resurrection power when I was in my teens. When I say 'met him' I mean experienced him in a profound life-changing kind of way. The kind of way that leaves you feeling blown apart but strangely whole. The Cris who sits writing this now is not the same Cris who existed moments before everything fell into place. Since then I have grown to love this thing called Christianity, but have also grown to feel that the whole system isn't working. I and friends of mine have been journeying in leaving religion behind to re-find the Jesus we met when we first fell in love with him; to find the Jesus that blew us apart and made us whole; to find the Jesus that gave us life.

When I first fell in love with Jesus I had a deep sense of joy, amazement, hope and passion, but over time religious behaviour crept in and all those good things seemed to get squeezed out. Please don't get me wrong; I am committed to the church, but I am not sure the church is always committed to Jesus and I don't always see his resurrection power being outworked in these communities. It's almost like there is a lack of connection to the power source.

Sometimes, it seems to me that people have turned up to this thing called church out of a sense of legality. If you don't turn up you will be thrown out of the 'Jesus club' or some club perks will be restricted: 'I'm so sorry, sir, but the parking is only for the committed card holders!'

People preach and you sit and quietly listen in the hope that something might be helpful, and that you don't fall asleep. But the Jesus I read about has words that bring people life and hope, not condemnation. His words of 'go and sin no more' and 'go in my peace' were always about freeing people from religious behaviour and language.

Home of the movement

I had the brilliant privilege of spending Easter 2008 in Jerusalem, seeing people getting ready for Jewish festivals, praying at the Western Wall and visiting one possible site of Jesus' tomb. The good news was the tomb was empty, Jesus had risen, and on Easter Day I joined thousands of people to worship at the Garden Tomb with the sun rising above us. After the service I had a short conversation with a local guy, where I commented on how fantastic it was to see so many local residents of Jerusalem out to worship on Easter Day. It turned out that the guy I was speaking to was a local Christian who served at a house that gave hope and care to Muslims who were disabled. He turned to me and very gently said, 'This is the birthplace of the Jesus movement. You in the West simply domesticated it.' And he was right; we *have* domesticated it.

Busted

I survived church up to my teens and stuck it out solely because I had nothing better to do. At 15, things weren't going quite as I'd planned. One night, friends and I decided to run home from a youth event down the estate using the fences and bushes in the residents' gardens as something to jump over. Imagine the Grand National over   people's gardens and you've got the idea. We called this 'garden hopping', others simply call it trespassing. We ran down the main length of the estate in record time, so a friend of mine decided to keep going onto the second stretch of the road. We had never jumped this section before and it was new territory so, with hearts pumping with adrenaline, we jumped over bushes and larger fences using bins as springboards and shrubberies as landing mats. One of my friends approached a set of bushes around 6 feet high and, using the bonnet of a car, he cleared the height. Following behind I tried to do the same, but sadly with little success. I jumped onto the bonnet and sprung right into the thickest part of the wall of evergreens.

I pause in the story, as on that fateful night there too was a pause.

When jumping into the bush I banged my head and landed out cold on the ground. My friends had run off down the hill. Meanwhile, the owner of the house, car and bush had rung the police. I came round with an old man and a police officer standing over me. There was no way out, I had been caught. Caught not 'garden hopping', but trespassing.

Are there times in your life when one thing after another goes wrong? With the months running up to the summer nothing could go right. School wasn't going great, I was caught doing lots of silly things, graffiti-ing the side of a train, drinking cider in the park . . . and did I mention trying to derail a train using two pence pieces?

Life hit a low.

Then summer came and I spent some time with Christian friends, camping, and they seemed to have it all together, or at least more than I did. They also talked about Jesus in a way that I couldn't understand. Jesus, to me, was some distant figure whose death had little significance to me, you could say *no* significance – it had been magic, after all. But their understanding of him somehow brought them life; they had life in their eyes that I couldn't understand. I didn't love Jesus in any shape or form, but at this point, seeing what they had, I wanted to love Jesus. Maybe saying that is a little strong; I probably wanted to want to love Jesus. I sat with my friends and explained how I wanted what they had and they prayed for me, and this felt right and good. I prayed that if there were a God that he would help me want to know him and even want to love him.

The change in me happened overnight; things fell into place and now I could find the point in so many of the pointless things I had seen in my previous churchgoing. This Jesus was alive and I could argue so because he was healing me and putting me back together. This healing didn't just come from knowing my sin was forgiven, but because Jesus' resurrection brought me life. I have come to realize that this resurrection has so much more power than I could ever imagine. In the years following these events, I have also come to realize that religion and Christianity are linked to Jesus, but they aren't Jesus.

Do you ever get this feeling that there has to be more than tea and biscuits, long sermons and, dare I say, the Bible? I am an orthodox Christian, I am also a 'priest', but I am longing for a deeper reality of Jesus. I look around and what I see is a mess. Lives lost and longing for direction, dysfunctional families, young people abusing their bodies, adults abusing their bodies. Is anyone sorted any more, or has the world gone crazy?

Wrestling with God

I met with a member of my church a few weeks ago. They told me about their world, their friends, how they see themselves, how they see family, how they hate their body and how they have had enough of their life. I sat across the table from them and was struggling to hold it all together; I simply wanted to cry for them. My heart is breaking for the people I walk past in the street, the people across from me on the Tube, or alongside me in the queue at the music store. The world is falling apart and this thing called Christianity simply seems to sit back and watch from the safety called church. We sit back and almost call for people to join us in our ivory tower with all its hymns, songs and sermons, but never offer anything to help change their world.

I have been wrestling for some time now with God, some-times angry at him and sometimes angry at the 'church' for not having anything to offer the brokenness of this world. It seems to me that the system isn't working, and we need to re-evalu-ate what is happening and who we are. This wrestling I have been doing with God recently has been leaving me walking with a limp; I am the one who is coming out with the injury, not God, and this book is the response to my wrestling.

There is a story in the Bible about a guy called Jacob who had been running for his life. The path his life had taken him on hadn't quite worked out to plan, and now he was running to find another way to live out his remaining years. One night, this heavenly being came to him and started a wrestling match with him right there in the dirt. The fight went on all night as Jacob wrestled intensely with the being. When the being realized he could not overpower Jacob, he touched his hip and wrenched it, and then had the cheek to demand that Jacob let him go as the sun was coming up. Jacob, knowing that this being was, in fact, some divine person, clung onto him and demanded a blessing from him before he let him go. As I said above, I have been wrestling with God for some time and have been walking with a limp as I have grappled with my frustrations, but through this wrestling and fighting I have found that God has blessed me, opening my eyes to a better way of seeing the whole system of religion; a better way of seeing his resurrec-tion community called the church.

I have come to the conclusion that I want to leave religion behind and become a follower of Jesus. Not a follower of a denomination, even though I am a part of one. Not a follower of a particular line of theology or style of worship, but a *follower of Jesus*. For too long I have found my religion not to be a thing which pushes me forward, but a thing which has held me back from truly getting to the heart of this Jesus movement. I want to encourage you to join me in wrestling with the movement called

Christianity. You might come away with your hip out of joint, but the holding on could mean that you are blessed and have your eyes opened to a new life, and a new way of living.

1.

The Alternative

Some emergent types want to recast Jesus as a limp-wrist hippie in a dress with a lot of product in His hair, who drank decaf and made pithy Zen statements about life while shopping for the perfect pair of shoes. In Revelation, Jesus is a prize-fighter with a tattoo down His leg, a sword in His hand and the commitment to make someone bleed.

Mark Driscoll in Relevant *magazine, March 2008*

Four foot fluffy neon pink cross

I have in my office a 4-foot high fluffy neon pink cross. It's not the standard image of the cross of Jesus, but is a stark reality that many of us simply see the cross as something cuddly to hold on to. The Christianity we recognize is often miles away from the Jesus we find in history. We interpret the Bible within our culture through our own values, our understanding of wealth and how life works. When we speak of the cross, it becomes a cuddly event in history where our friend Jesus died for us. It's distant, and easy to repaint the events in our minds to make them easy to stomach. The reality is gritty, dark and disturbing but also rich, beautiful and revolutionary. To understand the depth of the resurrection and the message it is communicating, we need to first understand who Jesus was and why his message was so challenging in the face of the empire.

If you were to ask a regular person on the street about who Jesus was or what he was like, they might say things like he was a good person or a bit of a hippie. Others would associate him with the blue-eyed, blond-haired, sash-wearing beauty queen – the standard unhelpful comments people normally make.

Holy revolutionary

Jesus was no hippie with sandals, but a holy revolutionary who came into a world that was divided, both economically and religiously. You were either living in extreme poverty or one of the wealthy; happily living in avoidance of the real situation. Religiously, you were in the group who were pushing forward in becoming more devout and holy while not caring about the world falling apart, or you were in the group that just didn't feel like it was working. The religious believers in Jerusalem were seeking God experiences, holiness and cleanliness to gain his approval. They would spend hours in worship reading the Torah, their holy Scriptures, praying devoutly for change and tithing more and more, in the hope of being seen by the Almighty YHVH. And while this was happening, the world outside of the religious centre was going to hell, it was falling apart and the religious people were simply sitting back. Aren't we glad we don't behave like this?

Understanding the historical setting and political backdrop of the world that Jesus broke into can help us to begin to see the beauty of Jesus' revolution and the depth, width and height of his resurrection.

Most revolutions are fought with military equipment, guns, and political and physical power. It's about the underdogs building up enough strength to take on the oppressive regime, which often means military fighting military. What is more important to note is that the Jews were expecting a military Messiah; they, too, were waiting for someone to come and fight for them. Jesus presented the Jews and the world with a new way of fighting.

Few Christians see the true depth of Jesus' revolution. This revolution undermined every single structure of power that the world had seen; the only way of dealing with the violent was to take on the violence, challenging it with your own life.

I have a friend who is a 'nice guy', he has always been a nice guy, and for a while we called him 'Nice Guy Eddie' after a character in a Quentin Tarantino film that at the time we thought was funny. It's strange how our humour changes. Some years ago, this friend and I were leading a youth event, and those planning it with us wanted to do a drama about Jesus. Soon the discussion moved to who would play the part of Jesus, and it was unanimous that my friend would do it. When the group was asked, 'Why him?', their response was, 'He's nice, like Jesus.'

Jesus was nice?

One dictionary definition says nice is 'someone or thing pleasing and agreeable in nature, having pleasant temperament. May exhibit courtesy and politeness. Of good character and reputation, respectable.' (HarperCol-lins General English Dictionary, 1995.)

I'm not sure Jesus was nice in the way our culture thinks he was. I cannot believe that Jesus standing up against the religious establishment, turning tables over in the Temple, hanging out with the detestable tax collectors and prostitutes and telling stories about those racist Samaritans points to a nice, clean-cut, sash-wearing Jesus. Don't get me wrong, I think he was good, I also think he was perfect – but 'nice' sounds just too neat and well-groomed.

Many of us act like Jesus was a nice guy, always saying his please and thank yous, teaching encouraging sermons and asking people to love each other; 'Just feel the love, man,' like some well-earthed surfer.

I find it absorbing that if this is how many of us see Jesus, how come we struggle to do this simple command, love one another (John 13:34)? We're able to do it on a Sunday but often seem to miss out the other six days. It's like an anti-Sabbath every day.

Jesus spoke about loving our neighbour, but so many of us don't even know our neighbours. Jesus was being provocative when he spoke about living in love, but we're so able to pick and choose who we love! We make it all about being nice.

Jesus' teaching was never nice. It was something gritty, challenging and new-world forming. His teaching was also political. Not the type of politics we see happening in parliament, but a politics that was about the day to day; it was about people and it was about freedom. Jesus spoke into the political world of the Roman Empire, and into an apathetic religious world drenched by conformity.

Jesus' teaching was about standing up and challenging the system head-on; it was a fearless revolution. He spoke about non-tolerance of double standards and hypocrisy, non-tolerance of oppression of the weak and young. He spoke of a group of people whose job was to bring liberation to the most crushed by the Empire, and a movement towards a new world order.

Nice, or awesome?

So what was really going on?

We need to start right back at the middle. Julius Caesar was assassinated on 15 March 44 BC leaving as his heir to the whole Roman Empire his nephew Augustus, who had been adopted as his son. Caesar Augustus came into power at a young age but this didn't stop him building the Roman Empire into a military power that could not be defeated by anyone. The Roman Empire with its trade routes and influence went from England all the way over to India. This empire was strong and needed nothing, it crushed cultures with no thought but its own gain, and at the centre of this was the Caesar. Caesar believed that the world needed changing; it was made up of weak cultures that fought amongst themselves. At one time Augustus described those outside the Empire as like bickering children and believed that someone needed to lead this chaotic world.

Caesar believed that he had the military power to build something new, something that would bring peace and harmony to the world. Caesar Augustus considered himself the 'Son of God' and was referred to as such. By this time, it was generally considered that Julius Caesar was a god and that his spirit had been seen going up into the heavens on his death. Hence his son was the 'Son of God' and both were worshipped as divine, with whole weeks of the Roman calendar set aside to celebrate their godhead. This message was communicated throughout the Roman Empire through political slogans which were stamped on coins and used in greetings. One such greeting was 'Caesar is Lord'. One famous refrain was, 'There is no other name under heaven by which people can be saved than that of Caesar.' Others called Augustus the 'prince of peace' and spoke of him being sent by the gods to bring about a universal reign of peace not just in the empire, but also in the whole world. People were forced to confess that Caesar was Lord and those who didn't were crucified in mass killings. All in all this worked, and the empire enjoyed peace for a time, known as the *Pax Romana*, or Roman peace.

It sounds breathtaking, doesn't it – one world leader believed to be divine, God on earth, ruling as he should be?

There were large divisions in the society of the empire, with male citizens of Rome at the top of the order and women and slaves at the bottom. There was nothing fair or equal about the way the empire was run; everyone knew that there was someone above them who could ultimately give him, or her, the chop.

Citizenship was also a central ethos of the Roman Empire. Almost in the same way some people are proud of the American flag, British Empire or their football team, people were proud of their Roman citizenship. The question when Rome invaded you was, were you going to join in, calling yourself a citizen? Caesar Augustus made it the law for all loyal Roman citizens to enter into emperor worship by burning a pinch of incense to Caesar, a practise that was imposed on and off right up to the fall of Rome in AD 476.

Caesar Augustus became strong very quickly and had, through military force, claimed Jerusalem for the empire. He then installed Herod as a Jewish client king, taking the power from the Jews who had originally governed the city. A client king was almost like a puppet king, not much real power, but had all the glory of a full king. Herod was always aware that he had to keep the empire happy, or he too would lose what he had.

Herod and the building projects

The wealthiest of the time had homes within the walls of Jerusalem where it was safe, and the poor lived outside the city in small villages with basic humble dwellings. These small villages were made up of people doing their best to survive, looking after sheep, growing whatever crops they could or making bread or oil. Bethlehem was just such a place, with people literally living off the ground. Everyone was fearful of the Romans and Herod because of their ridiculously high taxation and their violent behaviour which, at times, was inconsistent.

Herod the Great, half-Jewish and half-Edomite, was a fearless leader who did anything to keep his rule over his kingdom. He was powerful – some would say mentally unstable – and before becoming king was a violent military leader well known for massacring those in his way. The history books document Herod as killing his wives (he had about ten) and many of his children (he had around forty-three) purely because he was paranoid that they wanted him dead for his money and power.

Herod taxed the Jewish people alongside the Roman Empire, reducing them to poverty purely so that he could build his marvellous kingdom. He built temples (Second Temple in Jerusalem), amphitheatres, theatres, racecourses, seaports out in the sea (Caesarea Maritima), palaces on sides of mountains (Masada), palaces on mountains where there hadn't been mountains (Herodium), sewage systems and water systems. He built with such massive stones that even today we don't know how he lifted or moved them. He was an oppressor who did things simply so that he could impress the world. Some historians believe that proportionally he was probably one of the richest men in the world 'ever'.

Herod had around five hundred and fifty thousand people on his payroll; he built huge structures in places where it was impossible to build. On one occasion, Herod chose a location to build a fortress but there wasn't a mountain in that location so he had his own mountain shipped in (don't ask me where he found an unused mount). On this he created a palace, which he creatively called Herodium. This palace had a pool within it so large that Herod had to put an island in the centre so that you could swim to the middle and have a break before you carried on. It isn't documented that Herod ever used this pool; he built it because he could.

Caesarea Maritima has been described as one of the greatest engineering wonders of the world. It was the first major engineering projects to use concrete which would set under the water. The largest block measures 15 metres by around 11.5 metres, which is the length of a London bus. These blocks were created by floating a mould on the water and filling it with concrete; when it filled up it sank into place and then set under water. On one occasion, Herod was on a boat arriving at his seaport when he decided it wasn't beautiful enough, so he ordered his men to clad the whole entrance with gold to make it more pleasing to his eye. Not pleasing to everyone's eye, but *his* eye. He wanted to ride in on his boat and see the most beautiful seaport he had ever seen.

Herod built big projects in unrealistic locations so that he would be known as the kind of king who could build these things. He did it to make a name for himself and to gain approval from the Caesar. These building projects and the empire-building cost vast amounts of money and the only way both men could afford their craving for power was to tax the people for whatever they could. It is believed that at times they taxed the people 80 to 90 per cent of their money, food and cattle. If you were to go fishing, when you came back 80 to 90 per cent of whatever you had caught would be taken from you. If you had a bad night on the lake, it was tough. If you didn't have enough for your family to live on, it was tough. If you were starving to death and you were being taxed 80 to 90 per cent the only way out was to sell whatever you had in the hope of keeping afloat; sometimes this meant selling your daughter to be a prostitute or your son to be a slave.

The people were starving to death, struggling to make ends meet, crying out for a saviour. The empire was literally killing people while it was getting stronger. Herod was starving people while he gold-clad his seaport just so he could say it was the most beautiful he had ever seen. The system was sick and it was becoming terminal.

The world was a mess and the men who were focused on power and wealth were leading this mess. When individuals are focused on power and money they need to defend it because they know that they don't really have the ability to protect themselves. They have it now, but they have to keep themselves on top or they will lose it all.

Keeping on top

To do this, the Romans created a military force that would not be reckoned with; if anyone didn't go their way, they were simply eliminated. They also protected themselves with mass illustrations of authority, so often the empire would create opportunities to overtly show its strength. On one occasion, Augustus brought out his prisoners and paraded them around the street just to show and remind everyone of his military might.

And it is this world that Jesus was born into. A world that was about politics, money, wealth, manipulation, about taking as much as you could and the size of the growing military. It was a world focused on 'me and my needs', one that said, 'Who cares about those other people? I have my own problems.' It was a world focused on climbing up the ladder of success, building that extension so that 'I might feel more powerful'.

Jesus came into this world to show a way of building a kingdom focused on

Generosity not accumulation
Love not manipulation.

A kingdom that was

not about being your own god, but submitting to the God.

Two brothers

There is a story found in Genesis 27 about twin brothers. One is the hunter-gatherer and the other, the mother's boy. In this story the stronger son, Esau, is born first; therefore, he is lined up to receive the father's land, money and power when he dies. But before this happens in the story, the weaker brother, Jacob, tricks his father into giving him the family blessing. Jacob runs away to protect himself from his lie and then later bumps into the God who wrestles with him (remember that from the intro?). This story is about two brothers struggling for power; the naturally stronger one looks like he should have the power and wealth, but the younger one takes the power because God destined him to have it.

The naturally weaker brother is stronger because of God.

Jacob has children who then become God's chosen people, Israel. Israel is the family line from which Jesus comes later in the story. Esau, too, has children, and his family line is called Edomite. Remember earlier when I said Herod was an

Edomite? I bet you were wondering about that, weren't you?

Jesus comes from Jacob
Herod comes from Esau

The writer of the Gospel of Matthew starts his retelling of the events by reminding us that Jesus comes from Jacob, and then in chapter 2 says: 'After Jesus was born in Bethlehem . . . during the time of King Herod' (v. 1). The writer is reminding the reader that these two men have a history; like the two brothers Jacob and Esau there is a natural leader and there is a new leader arriving to take the power. Jesus arrives on the scene as an alternative king. Did I tell you that Herod called himself the 'King of the Jews'? Now there is a new king in town. We find out a little later in Matthew that the whole of Jerusalem was disturbed by Jesus' birth. Why was this? Why were they worried about a child? It was because they knew a new leader was coming, a leader of a new world order, an order where the poor lived in God's city.

Thirty

After thirty years, Jesus starts his attack against the empire and it is here that the fun starts. Much of Jesus' teaching has a political slant, or at least a subversive slant, towards his world order. An order where the poor are really the rich, and the rich are the poor.

On one occasion, Jesus was approached by Pharisees (Jewish religious leaders who lived by a very strict code of holiness) who came and warned him that Herod was looking to kill him whenever he could. Jesus' response was comical. Jesus said, 'Go tell that fox, "I will drive out demons and heal people today and tomorrow, and on the third day I will reach my goal"' (Luke

13:32). This, to us, seems like an irrelevant response, but to those hearing 2,000 years ago, this was full of political comedy. A fox was a symbol of weakness, lies and deception. A king was usually represented as a lion or a strong eagle, but a fox is a wannabe lion. Foxes prowl and lurk, hiding from anything making a noise, worried they're going to be caught. Foxes tend to come out at night and do their thing away from those who can question them.

I have a compost heap in my garden where we put all out-rvegetable waste; the plan is when it's composted we will use it next year on the next lot of veggies. Most days when I come to put new peelings in I find fox poo on the ground and scratch marks on the wooden composter where it has tried to get in. Never have I seen the fox, but on one occasion I knew it was hiding down the side of the shed waiting for me to leave so that it could have another go at getting to the part-rotten veggies. One night, the fox broke into my son's garden toy box and played with his footballs, so when Isaac came outside the next day some had bite marks and were burst. Never will the fox come out during the day so we can catch it; it only prowls around causing problems at night, knowing that we aren't there. Foxes basically find their food foraging in the streets and through people's waste compost or rubbish. They would certainly have been found living on and around the city rubbish dump called Gehenna, which Jesus in Matthew 5:29 uses as an image for hell (see also Mark 9:43). In fact, most Bibles now simply translate Gehenna as hell and don't even try to let us understand what Jesus was culturally referencing here. Jesus was painting the picture of Herod hanging out in the place of death and destruction.

Jesus associates Herod with a fox that will never come out head-on, but only deals in mischievous, undermining events when you aren't there, and lives in a place of death and decay.

For us, the image may work better if we use the idea of a rat; Herod the dirty rat hiding in the sewer, coming up for food, and carrying germs.

Imagine the response in the crowd: 'Did you hear that Jesus called King Herod a lurking fox?' People were probably telling the story for weeks as some kind of joke. Imagine the school-children in the playground talking about the event like it was the latest *Doctor Who* episode, or the mumblings in the marketplaces. Whenever Herod was nearby some might even join in the mocking by shouting it, then running to hide. If Jesus hadn't already angered Herod, then now he would have; Jesus had made Herod a joke.

Jesus didn't merely set Herod up as being the other option or another way. Jesus highlighted that his approach was completely different to that of Herod's empire and power.

White stallions and small BMXs

In Mark 11:1–11, we read a story about Jesus parading into Jerusalem on the back of a colt or young donkey. It is often taught that this was simply a parade to fulfil the prophecies in Zechariah 9. However, as with a lot of what Jesus did, there is much more going on than meets the eye. Many of the Gentile onlookers wouldn't have known the prophecies but would have understood what they saw.

On a normal day there could be around forty thousand pilgrims within the walls of Jerusalem for worship. However, once a year during Passover the numbers could rise to around one hundred and forty thousand. There was no room for all these people to stay in Jerusalem, so some would stay in little villages surrounding the holy city, such as Bethany and Emmaus. But those who couldn't find space there – or lacked the necessary finances or family contacts – would camp out on the Mount of Olives overlooking the holy city. For many visiting Jews, their holy city had been contaminated by the presence of the unclean Roman leaders. Many of the Roman soldiers had been employed from the surrounding area, not from Rome, some came from the poor north and others from Samaria. Many of the Roman soldiers were in fact 'those dirty and unclean' Samaritans that the Jews hated with a deep, deep racist hate. All of this crowding, racism and hate of the empire created a volatile situation. In the past, large fights would break out, causing the city to fall into chaos. In response to this, Rome put on a demonstration of its force and power to remind Jerusalem who was really in charge of the holy city.

Most of the time, Pilate lived on the Mediterranean coast in Herod's beautiful city, Caesarea Maritime. Here life was easy and, with the beautiful views and cooling wind, it was a perfect place to live. Each year Pilate would make his way to Jerusalem and parade into the city from the west, revealing Rome's power and authority in a huge display involving copious amounts of Roman soldiers, large white stallions and the Imperial symbol, the eagle. It was large, it was loud, and it showed the Romans' presence in Jerusalem. Doing this put any fighting to rest and anyone who did cause problems was crucified as a sign to all that the Romans were really in charge.

It is historically believed that Pilate would arrive in the city of Jerusalem from the west on the first day of the week before the day of Passover; so he would arrive on the Sunday. Jesus also arrived in the city on the Sunday on the east side, over the Mount of Olives. (In John 12:1 we are told that Jesus arrived six days before Passover into a little place called Bethany – that would have been a Saturday. It then says in John 12:12 that the next day Jesus went onto Jerusalem on the donkey.) So, both Jesus and Pilate arrived in the holy city on the same day, which was Sunday. Could it be that Jesus' parade was a counter-parade making mockery of Pilates display of power and authority? We are told in the story that Jesus arrived in the city on a colt; a colt isn't an adult donkey, it's a young donkey. Jesus was riding into the holy city on a donkey that a child would ride at the same time as Pilate was on his beautiful white stallion.

A few weeks ago, I was in the park with my son, who was on his bike. After some time he had had enough and left me with his bike, which I decided to try to ride on. My son is 4 and his bike is small with stabilizers. I was having great fun trying to ride around until I realized how ridiculous I looked, a grown man on a child's bike. Jesus would have looked the same with his sandals scraping along the streets of Jerusalem.

In view of the empire's procession, Jesus' entrance takes on a deeper meaning. On the west was a parade about politics, authority, economics and military power, and on the east was a parade of life, joy, fun and love.

Jesus was setting himself up as an alternative to the empire, and this alternative wasn't just another flavour but a completely different option. Jesus was coming into the city as a counter-empire with no troops, no money, little authority or power – but coming in peace. Peace was the other option, and this would only be found in Jesus. Jesus' parade was a mockery of the whole Imperial system, an upside down empire willing to make fun of itself.

The system

Jesus' challenge wasn't just to Herod and the empire, it was to a whole system that the empire represented – the gods. The empire worshipped many different gods including the Caesars and, at various points in his teaching, Jesus' poked fun at them. There were two gods in particular that are interesting for us when looking at this topic.

The first is the god Tammuz, which means 'the true son' or 'the true son of god'. This god was believed to have power over food and vegetation. The Romans believed that each year he would wander the earth bringing life to crops, fields, flowers and plants. Everywhere he walked, life would spring up; when he died in the autumn, life no longer flowed from him. Then the following year in the 'third month', Tammuz would rise from the dead again, creating a rhythm called the 'dying-and-rising of the god Tammuz' or even the 'resurrection of Tammuz'. If Tammuz wasn't to resurrect each year, then food would not grow and there would be famine and death. The followers of Tammuz were very important, as their worship was the very thing that brought Tammuz back to life.

The second, and even more interesting, is the goddess Isis. This goddess was believed to be the ultimate grandmother of all the kings of Egypt with the bloodline going right back to the first king of the whole world, Assur. When Assur died it was believed that Isis resurrected him and he fathered the line of kings with her. Lots of leaders from Jesus' time were trying to trace their lineage right back to Assur and Isis. The name Caesar contains Assur: C+ Assur = Cassur, which became Caesar. Caesar believed he was linked right back to the blood of Isis, and therefore when Caesar died he too would be resurrected and given life eternal in heaven.

It was then believed that when Isis and Tammuz died they were resurrected too, and ascended into heaven with all the other gods; almost like a god 'green room' where they were all waiting for their next turn on the stage – gods waiting for their next turn on the stage called earth. They didn't do anything, they just sat watching, poking fun at and commenting on an earth they were distant and separate from.

The followers of Jesus saw their rabbi die and then claimed that they had seen him on the 'third' day, resurrected. They said that he had spent time proving his resurrection to them and had walked the streets teaching and preaching, bringing life to others, and that after forty days he had ascended up into heaven, not to be seated in the 'green room', but to be seated at the right hand of God himself. The 'right hand' was a phrase used by the followers which meant Jesus was sat at the power source of God; the right hand was the hand you would punch someone with, the hand of power, the hand of authority. Jesus had died but these followers made it clear that he had resurrected and ascended, not to the green room but to the power source of God. In other words, Jesus was the power of the universe.

The story didn't stop there. Unlike all the other gods waiting in the 'green room', Jesus made his presence known. He sent his power and authority in the form of a spirit and even spoke to Saul on the way to Damascus. Jesus never sat watching, poking fun at and commenting on the earth, but was involved in the lives of his followers, with his resurrection power working through them. His followers were now practising his resurrection power on the people they met in the Temple, on the street and in their homes. Jesus' death and resurrection was a direct comment on all the other gods. Jesus was revealing that he was the ultimate power and authority, and that his resurrection had universal implication. All the other resurrections were about the gods and how they could live forever in the 'green room', but Jesus' resurrection was a sign that death itself had been beaten and that he was inviting others into his resurrection power. The resurrection was no longer an event only the gods could enjoy, but now an event that any person could enjoy.

No nice guy

Jesus was never the 'nice guy'; he was the guy who challenged the whole power and authority system of death and anyone who was associated with it. Jesus' resurrection was poking fun at death, and using it to reveal his true power.

Caesar called villages or towns that chose to worship him ekklesia, which we would translate as church. Jesus gave Peter the job of starting his *ekklesia*; his *ekklesia* was to be Jesus' conduit or channel on earth, and the very way Jesus would reveal his resurrection to the empire. The church Jesus started was a group of people who had experienced the resurrection and were now calling others into it.

The church was an invitation into Jesus' resurrection. The church was Jesus' resurrection body on earth, and its role was to bring life.

Thinking deeper

- What is the Jesus like that you follow? Would you want to hang out for coffee or beer with him? How real and honest is he? How gutsy is he, how challenging? How does his grace extend to you?
- How do you see the empire around you? Are you happy living in the empires that surround you? Who is the modern day fox?
- If Jesus is the 'power of the universe', what does this do to the image of Jesus you have? How big does Jesus become, knowing that he challenged the power of the time and flipped it on its head to reveal his raw, true power?
- 'The naturally weaker brother is stronger because of God.' In Jacob and Esau's story the weaker brother becomes the stronger because he is clothed in his brother's role. You are stronger because you are clothed in Jesus. What way does this move you into a new life?
- How does this new life now spill over into the everyday?
- How have you seen the church being Jesus' resurrection body on earth? How can you play your role in this resurrection community of bringing life?

Example of resurrection: One

A real-life story about a person named Tom:

I can't complain, I grew up in a great home with my parents and experienced a good, positive home life. It wasn't the outside world that was causing me problems, it was my inside world. Deep down I didn't seem to know who I was; I felt like I was living someone else's life. I could tell you what I liked – playing sports, watching TV, hanging out with friends and going clubbing – but I didn't really have any identity for myself. I didn't have any confidence in who I was and had no security that I was OK and normal.

Life seemed to get more complicated when I tried to live by the rules unhelpful friends gave me. The society I lived in told me that I needed to earn money, get the car and have the new piece of technology in my pocket. It also told me that I needed a girlfriend and I needed to be having sex. Sex was the point of life, and without it I believed I was missing out on something. The solution to my mundane life was sex according to the world around me. I read too many magazines and was watching too much TV and this poisonous view of the world was screwing with my mind and eventually made me feel worse.

Throughout my teens, right up to hitting 22, the point of living was to try to have sex with whoever I could. I would only speak to girls I found attractive, girls I thought there was some possibility of having sex with. Life became more frustrating when all the girls I dated only ever wanted to stop at kissing. I chose the ones I thought had low self-esteem, the ones who looked desperate, and still they only wanted to stop at kissing.

Things weren't helped by my growing addiction to porn. Seeing those images on the computer and TV screen only made me want to have sex more. Each image ingrained on my mind made me want to find someone who would let me do that to them. The porn started to really play with my mind; I started to see the world differently and think that all plumbers got it on with the lonely housewife. I wasn't a plumber and I never met the lonely housewife. Women became objects for me to crave and I longed to see them naked. Masturbation became more than a simple pastime; it became a way of seeing the day through.

I was told the meaning of life was to get and enjoy sex, and as I wasn't getting any I did the next best thing. Over time it became an addiction; rarely did I go through a day without looking at porn, which made work difficult at times.

Life felt more like a prison than something I was free to enjoy. I was a slave to these attitudes, thoughts, views and images. Sex, masturbation and porn had become my Egypt and I needed a Moses to walk me to freedom.

Finally things were starting to drop into place, to the point where I seemed to be getting better at talking to women and was finally getting somewhere on the 'losing my virginity front'. For some reason I began to wonder whether or not this would make me happy. Even though I wanted to have sex, I always wanted a loving relationship; I never wanted sex to be separated from love. But my frustrations were eroding this belief. As I was getting close to finding someone to have sex with, I began to rethink.

When life hit a real porn low, a friend of mine asked me to go to church with him. It wasn't that he was a Christian and that he wanted to convert me, it was actually that he had heard that there was a local church where all the girls were hanging out. I needed space from desperately searching for sex and I thought that Christian women would stop me thinking about it. My idea of a Christian woman was frumpy with facial hair, definitely not someone I would want to be with. After putting it off and making excuses for weeks, I eventually got dragged along.

It was the wrong week to go because the talk was on . . . sex! The last thing I needed was some Christian   banging on about sex only being for marriage. I wanted to get it, not be put off from having it.

I realized that the talk wasn't on condemning me, or making me feel there was something wrong with me. It invited me into a new life, a new way of living that would make life more purposeful. As the person spoke, I had all the questions going around my mind answered.

It wasn't the message of sex that resonated with me; it was this guy's understanding of Jesus. I didn't like Christians, I thought they were judgemental hypocrites, but this Jesus character seemed to be an invitation into real life.

The speaker also said one of the most liberating things that made me rethink my view on life. He said Jesus never had sex; he never got married; yet he lived a fulfilled life. His friends surrounded him and he brought happiness to people, but never had sex. For him, sex   wasn't the meaning of life.

That was it! I made a commitment to not having sex before marriage. (And in subsequent weeks I made a full commitment to following this guy Jesus.) I decided sex was anything past kissing, as anything using the 'big gun' was a 'grey area', and I did not want to let God, myself or my future wife down by getting into any 'grey areas'.

From that night onwards I never looked at any porn ever again. By the help of Jesus and his resurrection power he rebuilt me, and repaired the damage the porn and I had made. I realized sex was not the meaning of life; the meaning of life was my status before God as a loved and forgiven son. This was possible because of Jesus' life, death, resurrection and ascension. God had given me his Spirit to show that I was in the Body of Christ.

God healed me from this addiction, and because of his unconditional love – which is my confidence – I was able to find out who I was, what makes me, *me*, and not to be ashamed of it, but accept that no one is perfect, Jesus died for me and his Spirit is helping me every second of my life.

The reality was that I realized I'd had lots of Christians around me most of my life. I had friends who behaved in a different way and this had made me turn to them for help on several occasions. They always just seemed like nice people who were willing to hear me talk through sex without being forceful with their ideas. Two or three of them had talked to me about how they were waiting to get married and I had avoided thinking about this until the night the preacher had my attention.

The reality hit me that it wasn't what the preacher said that helped me, but his words helped me see something different in the Christian friends I had around me. It was like he held a shining a light on them and suddenly their attitudes and lives looked very different.

This group of friends, surprisingly, had stuck by me when I was living in a narrow and confined view of the world. I realized that I had been living in slavery, chained to deformed ideas of sex, women and masturbation. I was also enslaved by porn, filling my mind with images that told me I wasn't a real man unless I could do that thing to a woman.

Jesus' resurrection power has worked and is still working in me. When I finally understood that God is concerned about the mess in this life, and he wants to help us, I realized why people told me Jesus loves me all those years ago. I was changed when I met Jesus and he has changed the way I look at life; he has shown me what life is about, and that what our society says about what will make us happy is usually wrong.

2.

The Problem

You are my very first and best love poem crafted from
my mouth.
Each syllable became a word of life and of breath.
My image is yours and will always be however it's
        abused.
I loved you and still love you.
My love is like a waterfall: cleansing, forgiving, over-
        flowing.
Now, I see your back, disappearing into the distance.
My heart is ripped to shreds, torn in two and there is
        pain.
Oh so much pain!
I gave you everything.
You gave me nothing.

As you slip through my fingers,
I cry, 'Come back to me my children, come back.'

'Lament' by Jared Lovell (2009)

Eloah is not Hawaiian

Before we get to grips with the true depth of Jesus' understanding of 'life' it is helpful to understand death, and for that we need to start right back at the beginning.

In the beginning God created the heavens and the earth and he said it was good. The third word in the Hebrew Scriptures is the word *Elohim* which traditionally we have translated as God, but there is much more going on in this title than at first reading, and many would argue that this is too simple a translation. The name *Elohim* is in fact a plural word from the singular word *Eloah*, which is rendered as 'the mighty and powerful one'.

So, *Elohim* is the plural version of *Eloah*, which means that the name of God used in the Genesis poem is a plural name; in other words, this name indicates that God was plural – and thus in relationship to someone else. But who is this someone?

Before anything existed, there existed *Elohim*. God – Father, Son and Spirit. All parts eternally seamlessly existing in what has been described as loving union so perfect, so beautiful, that the three are one. There is a word for this: *Perichoresis*. Some people have said that it is how these relate that blows our mind and have described it as 'an intimate shared indwelling' or you could say, a warm willingness to live in each other. Others have said that it is like a 'mutual dance' with all three Persons of the Trinity dancing together in time, each knowing the next move of the others before they have even got to the next move.

Dance

Have you ever been to a dance class? Have you ever seen the muppet at the back who has no idea what they are doing? This is probably me. I just don't get dancing, I enjoy it but I can't do it. I always, no matter what music, end up looking like a dad dancing. Out of time, arms all over the place hitting people like an out of control monster, with passers-by crying, 'Out of the way, it's coming though, ahhhhhhh!'

Then there is always the couple who dance so beautifully that it's almost as if they aren't two dancers but one – joined together, creating something fresh and new every time.

This is the image that people have used to describe God – like people dancing. A beautiful dance between three lovers, all equal, all humble, all perfectly relating, each being more aware of the others' moves than of their own.

I have problems describing the relationship between Father, Son and Spirit but I can see the dance and I get the dance, I can understand that.

Dust-man and the God who dances

It is from this relationship that creation flows. From this relationship of mutual respect that God creates. It was once taught by rabbis that in fact *Elohim* was 'Love' – not made of love, but was the heart of where love originated. And that from the very belly of *Elohim* a waterfall flowed into the world and this waterfall was love itself. In 1 John 4:16 the writer taps into this truth about God, saying that 'God is love, and the one who resides in love resides in God, and God resides in him' (NET). But what does this love look like? *Agape* is one of the Greek words for love. This isn't as simple as a human emotional buzz for someone attractive or intelligent. *Agape* is an unconditional, self-giving, active and vocal love. It is a love where you are always on that person's mind; nothing takes their attention away from you. You are on their radar 24/7.

God is the very existence of sacrificial, life-giving love; love flows into the world from him, and it was from this position that his creative passions flowed.

Anyway, back to the creation story. *Elohim* created the sun, moon, stars, earth, sea, air. He made creepy things and walking things, things with eyes and some without, some had fur and some had scales, some walked on feet and some he created to sit in their owner's handbags. And all of this he said was good.

Later in the poem found in Genesis 1, God decides to create people in his image. These people are to rule over the fish of the sea and birds of the air, over the cows and sheep and ox and all the other creatures that were on the ground. So God makes humanity in his 'image'. What is really interesting is that in the Genesis poem in verse 27 the writer repeats twice that God created humanity in his image: 'So God created man in his own image, in the image of God he created him'.

God didn't make humankind in the image of any other animal, nor did he create something from scratch; he, the creator God who has the power and imagination to make whatever he decides, chooses to use a pre-existing template for this being. This is a tested and well-crafted, perfectly formed template. This template is that of *Elohim* himself, the God who dances. I think the writer of Genesis is trying to tell the reader of this poem something, and this something has to do with how God is choosing to create this being.

In Genesis 3, we find that *Elohim* forms a man out of the dust of the ground, which in Hebrew is *adamah*. The Hebrew for man is 'Adam'; a closer way of translating 'Adam' is ground man, or dust-man. We are dust-men and women!

The story goes on that God then takes this lifeless dust body and breathes his life into the being. The word for breath is *ruach*, often this is translated as Spirit; so *Elohim's* breath is also his Spirit, and it gives dust-man life. The very breath of the creator God pumps life into the heart of dust-man. The rabbis taught that the body was only kept alive because the Spirit of *Elohim* was moving inside of it and that once the life-force left the person they were dead. We know that we are alive because of a heart that is beating with blood pumping around and our lungs drawing air in and out. But if you have ever seen someone you love when they are dead, you can't help but notice that there is something different, much more than simply the body no longer pumping blood. We would say the soul, or their spirit, has left them, the shell is now empty.

There are other creation accounts found in the Bible, two in Genesis and five others dribbled through the Old Testament (check out the one in Job 38 where God lists his amazing creation. God is essentially saying to his reader, 'Have you seen my creation lately?'). But there are other creation stories, sometimes called myths, found in the Middle East. One is the Babylonian creation myth which tells the story of Marduk who creates the world not out of love but anger, and that he creates humans and chooses to place his spirit in one special human, the king. It was believed in Babylon that only royalty had the god's spirit in them and therefore they were the earthy representation of the god Marduk. This idea of the gods' placing their spirit in special human beings was standard at the time of Moses and before.

So the creation story of Genesis 1 was groundbreaking, it was years ahead of those religions. This story of Genesis said that God chose not to put his Spirit in one or two people, but that he chose to breathe his Spirit into all people. All of his children held within them his breath that gave them life. Every human, therefore, was God's representative, everyone was 'in' and everyone was both physical and spiritual.

We are fragile dust-men and women who exist not because of our own power but because *Elohim* has breathed his ruach, his life-giving breath into our dry bodies.

The story then continues that *Elohim* takes the rib of dust-man and creates dust-woman and then tells them that they have a free rein of this beautiful garden he has called Eden. *Elohim* then gives them one rule, pause . . . He actually gives

Adam a few rules, firstly to look after the garden and take care of it; he then commands him to eat from the trees. It was a command, not a suggestion, to enjoy the garden and the food found within it. Dust-man is also told to unite with his wife, that's an order! And within all these positive rules he gives the rule to not eat from the tree of knowledge of good and evil. This rule to not eat, I would argue too, was a positive rule, a rule to keep dust-man and woman safe.

We all know how the story goes and dust-man and dust-woman both eat from the tree and they get sent from the garden for ever. Paradise is lost.

Chatta't

In Genesis 4 we are then introduced to a new Hebrew word, *chatta't*. *Chatta't* is roughly said like a deep Russian voice with lots of intense emotions, it's not a light word or a word that would make you smile, but a very deep, serious word.

This word has many ideas tied into it. Firstly, *chatta't* is something that brings death, but this death isn't just the separation between our souls and our physical bodies, but also our souls becoming separated from God. *Chatta't* brings a total, destructive death that can't be rewound; it destroys individuality and makes uniformity; everything becomes bland in *chatta't*. It also stops someone from seeing God's realm and undermines everything that is good in the world. *Chatta't* undermines God's politics of justice for the poor, builds its own kingdom and is associated with a legal transaction with someone you're in debt to. If the rabbi that once described God as having the waterfall of love flowing from his belly into the world was correct, then *chatta't* is the black hole which draws in this love and destroys it. *Chatta't* is the antidote to love and life.

One atom of *chatta't* causes destruction to the whole created order and causes chaos. *Chatta't* affects all aspects of our lives; it changes the way we see the world and others around us. *Chatta't* grows like a cancer, slowly and silently taking over bit by bit.

We translate the word *chatta't* as sin. I don't know about you, but when I hear the word sin, or the word sinner, I cringe. It's been hijacked by street preachers and fundamentalists who shout the word out at every conceivable moment like spiritual Tourette's telling the world how much a sinner it is. It's not that they are wrong, we are all sinners, but this word has lost all impact. We don't see how this sin really has any effect on the world. For a world which has become cynical about Christians, cynical about church and cynical about Jesus, this word has lost any reality.

This understanding of *chatta't*, which we bring into the world by our actions, then starts to pin us down and hold us back. It becomes a legal contract between Satan and us. He now owns us, and the world's response is . . . so what? It's like there is no real understanding of this concept any more; it's almost like someone who knows that they have blown their long-term relationship, thinking there's no way back, so they don't even try to redeem it.

Out of control

The office I use to write in is a small box room with books on three walls, there are books piling up on the floor, and books on books on the shelves. The bins haven't been emptied in weeks and are now starting to overflow and there are cables and sheets of paper stacking up on the workspace. I have a small area large enough for my keyboard in the centre of the desk, and the rest is overflowing. There is a filing cabinet by the door that hasn't been used by me for filing for years, or at least, my filing is better described as stuffing things in.

I never intended it to get this messy, there wasn't a specific moment where I realized it was getting this awful. Over time it just got unpleasant. There was a time when it looked immaculate and it was an office to be proud of, but now even my wife will not go in. Have you ever experienced a room like this? For some of my friends it's the inside of their car. Things start to pile up and take over fast. My problem is that it's so bad I don't have the energy to do anything about it; it's easier to just push it all back and create enough space to work, avoiding the mess.

The world is in a mess but all we want to do is push back the papers, restrain the falling books and pretend everything is going to plan.

The black and white law

Many just see sin as a term used by the religious to describe any act that violates a moral code or rule. Sin is seen as an action that is prohibited by a higher force, an action that breaks a particular ruler's law. People see God as this cosmic rule-maker who sets the world up to fail because it simply can't attain the standard that he wants. Others see sin as a legal violation or a contract abuse, which means salvation is about remaking the contract.

Our experience of the law is a set code which we need to live by or we will be arrested, imprisoned and, in some parts of the world, given the death sentence for. It is black and white, rules are either broken or not. And the one who administers this law is seen as a higher party who needs to be above the law. The problem with this system is that we want to kick against it; we see the law as unfair and those who administer it to somehow be avoided, and demonized.

I recently got a letter from the police telling me that I was caught on camera driving at 37 mph in a 30 mph limit area and that I was to get a fine and points on my licence. The letter was able to tell me when and where I speeded and I was able to remember doing it and the flash of the camera. Even though I knew I had done this, I started to get all self-righteous, telling myself that I was speeding because this happened or it was that other car's fault; I even started to argue that the road was inadequately signed with the speed.

I was like the child who has been caught taking one too many biscuits and is searching for any excuse to make themselves feel better.

I was found speeding and there are others like me who are caught doing maybe 50 mph in a 30 mph area by a police officer; they naturally try to worm out of it as if the police are some kind of gang which needs to be dodged. There are other times like this with parking attendants who try to keep the roads clear of obstruction. We like them doing their jobs when they keep the roads free from those who should not park there, but when it's us parking badly we try to dodge the ticket.

Demonizing the cosmic Judge

We demonize those who try to keep the law and, in the same way, we demonize God in trying to keep his law. We expect him to be this cosmic Judge who we need to try to dodge, and if we can do this by avoiding believing in him, what better way of getting away with it? 'Sorry, officer, I didn't even know you existed, so how was I supposed to know that I needed to drive carefully on the road?'

For centuries, the church has made sin simply about an individual understanding. I am a sinner; therefore, Jesus' death sets me free. The problem is that *chatta't* is much bigger than just individual sin. *Chatta't* is the whole created order dying a painful death, being made bland, falling into chaos.

Chatta't is growing in the world like a cancer, slowly and silently taking over bit by bit.

Systemic dimensions

The church talks about individual sin, but we need to see that *chatta't* has a systemic dimension. Systemic simply means that there are systems and patterns of sin in the world which our own personal *chatta't* plays into and feeds.

The mess of the world is not happening due to an overarching divine punishment or attack, but because there is this huge tragedy happening due to forces beyond human control or even comprehension, all stemming from human greed, human lusts for sex, money and power. There is a lack of care for the natural order all coming from our own selfishness, seeing ourselves as the most important.

We in the West have, in our collective smug worlds, somehow come to the conclusion that we are mini gods; we have become like a day-dreaming nation, all high on our own self-importance. Our technology, power and wealth have separated us from the reality of the world around us. We have become skilled at avoiding the real world, which has become an addiction in itself.

The truth is that we can't avoid the reality of the world. We might buy the safest car, but it doesn't stop the accidents occurring. We might buy the newest designer shoes, but it doesn't stop us feeling lonely. We might have the newest phone, but still be unconnected to people around us. We might have air conditioning or heating, and be disconnected from the seasons. We might have the newest MP3, and be disconnected from the soundtrack God created.

Chatta't separates us from love. What if love looks like community, people sitting together chatting, singing communal songs? What if love looks like creation and God's personal soundtrack of the birds, wind and rain? Have you ever stood in the rain, feeling the drops on your face? Have you ever felt so alive other than when you're connected to creation? Love looks like connection to God, people and creation.

We have corporately assumed that we have total control of the world, mastering all the areas of life, death, health, money, security, flight, communication, space travel and consumption. The hard truth is that we can't control the world, nature, other people or even aspects of ourselves. We can't fix everything quickly and easily and we can't have everything we want just because we want it.

Systemic sin is when, over a long period of time, something has crept into bigger structures and societies. It is where the very structure of the organization or community is designed in such a way that it is innately sinful – for example, where the structures are built to pervade racism, sexism, religious hatred, enforce poverty of some, and other forms of prejudice and discrimination.

Systems of bias

Some politics have a bias to the rich, others discriminate against single parents or the elderly. Some practises are undoubtedly there for the benefit of the upper classes at the expense of the poor. Some organizations are built around a belief system of hierarchy that ranks people according to their economic status, family line and skin colour.

There are many more examples of systems that are biased like this, and I am sure you can see them around you every day. For instance, the greedy seeking profit from the poor – and those seeking power at the cost of those around them, which means they even destroy necessary natural resources or allow second-rate building safety for their own gain. We recently heard a loud explosion late at night; we found out the next day that the home of a family not far from us had been burnt to the ground with two people inside. It turned out that the gas work done in the house was below standard; it had been done as cheaply as possible. The lives of people are put at stake each day because someone else wants to cut corners to make more money.

What about political parties that are only interested in keeping themselves in power and do so by ignoring difficult issues, refusing to see the problems for the poor, the marginalized, the school systems or in health care? Some politicians do not acknowledge the needs of others and seem only to care about their own fame and glory.

What about the systems of sin which we call 'our right'? It is my right to choose to drive a petrol guzzling 4x4 even if it will affect the lives of future generations. It is my right to have a huge house for all my stuff, to show the world my status, when there are people dying of homelessness. It is my right to keep the money I earned – I worked hard for it. It is my right to keep the poor at arms' length. It is my right to build my factory or hotel wherever I like. It's not my problem that what I'm doing is damaging the environment or putting people at risk, as long as I have what I need and more. It's my right to have bigger, flashier, more expensive . . . don't worry about those people, they're not that important. It is my right to buy whatever clothes I want, even if a child makes them. It's my right to drink good coffee, even if the farmers get paid so little. It's my right to eat food out of season, even if flying it to me is burning up the earth's resources. It's my right to have ten pairs of boots when my neighbour has none. It's my right to bypass the deprived parts of town so as not to see those kinds of people.

Our rights have been used to uphold the rich and press down the poor. Our rights are a key part of this system of sin.

Jesus could see it

Jesus understood systemic dimensions to sin, and it was all around him. The Romans oppressed Israel to get what they wanted, men oppressed women, and vineyard owners used slave labour to work their farms. There are subtle comments to these systems throughout Jesus' stories and teachings.

One good example is that of the story of the Good Samaritan found in Luke 10:25–37. A man from Israel is walking on the road from Jerusalem to Jericho. It was a well-known road for ambushing and theft because of how winding it was. On route to Jericho, the man is attacked by a group of thieves and has everything he possesses taken from him. They steal all his belongings, even his clothes, and beat him, only leaving when they think he is dead.

In Jesus' story, he tells us three people walk by; a priest, a Levite and a Samaritan. But there is more going on in this story than we first think; this probably wasn't the first time the people have heard this story. Many rabbis used a similar one in teaching about the importance of regular people serving the poor. In their story, a priest and Levite walk by but the difference in their version is that a typical Jewish layman is the third person to walk by and not the Samaritan. In the original story, the layman walks by, helps the man up, and looks after him. In Jesus' story there was no layman – the third person was a Samaritan. The question is, why does Jesus change the story? The original was a good story about serving the poor. If his story is about helping people, then the original would have done the job for him; why bring in a Samaritan?

The truth is that Israel hated the Samaritans with a deep, racist hate. One Jewish book called *Mishna Sheveth 8,10* reads: 'He that eats the bread of the Samaritans is like to one who eats the flesh of pigs.' (The Jews saw pigs as an unclean evil animal which you would not dare to go near or touch.)

The Jewish writer, Ben Sirach, lived 200 years before Jesus, wrote: 'There are two nations I detest. The third is not a nation at all, the inhabitants of Mt Sear and the Philistines and the stupid people of Shechem.' Those stupid people at Shechem were the Samaritans. We start to paint a picture of what was going on at the time. We also know that sometime after Jesus, both the Samaritans and the followers of Jesus were publicly cursed in the synagogues, with prayer made asking that they would not inherit salvation. The Jews publicly prayed against people meeting their Creator.

Jesus' teachings were subversive; they flipped the whole world order upside down, placing it on its head. Jesus takes a story about serving the poor and those in need and turns it into a teaching about systemic racism. The very person the Jews hate is the one who now comes to save the near-dead man. The man's saviour is 'one of those stupid people of Shechem'.

Have we got caught up in holiness?

Does the church have any systems of racism or prejudice? What would we make of Jesus if he arrived in our church this coming Sunday and told us a story: In this story a man meets his doom one night on his way home from work. Next morning, the local preacher comes along, sees him and walks on by, then the local youth pastor walks by, and crosses the road. But then a gay guy walks past, helps him up and takes him to safety. Could it be that the church has become so caught up with the holiness issue like the Priest and Levite in the original story that someone who the church sees as 'unclean', 'not in the club', 'out', 'far off', 'sinner' is the one who comes and helps?

The church asks Jesus, 'Who is my neighbour?' and Jesus' response is, 'The guy the church keeps saying is out.' In the story there is no mention of the Samaritan's sin; for Jesus, his sin wasn't ever the issue of the story, it was the sin of Israel and their racist hate for the Samaritan people. Could it be that Jesus would be more disappointed with the church than he would be with someone who was gay?

Fig leaves

Back to the creation story, where dust-man and dust-woman bring *chatta't* into the world. Very quickly we see the effects of their actions; before eating the fruit we read in Genesis 2:25 that they were naked and felt no shame, but only a few verses later we read that their eyes were opened and they realized they were naked. Who saw them naked? They saw each other naked. There was no one else there, other than the snake.

The first thing that happens when *chatta't* enters the world is that relationships are broken; dust-man and woman no longer wish the other to see their nudity. It's almost as if they don't want the other to see what is really going on with them, they are now hiding the real them. The breakdown of relationships is right at the heart of the human problem, and the problem continues today. How many people have you spoken to, saying 'How are you?' and their reply is 'Good, thanks!', and you know it's not good, you know that there are things going on inside of them that aren't good? Each Sunday, I turn up to church and ask people, 'How's your week been?' and fig leaves go up and they avoid answering the questions.

How often do we hide what is really going on inside of us because we don't want people to know that everything isn't OK? We wear fig leaves to hide our true selves and this is a direct effect of *chatta't*. In this creation poem, the first act of sin was to destroy the very first relationships of humankind. The second was to then lie to the Creator himself by hiding from him, and we have been hiding ever since.

People sometimes say, 'If there is a God, then why does he choose to hide?' or 'I can't believe there is a God. I can't see him.' Maybe it's not God hiding, maybe it's us hiding from him?

Falling apart and out of control

After dust-man and woman have left the garden they have children, and in Genesis 4 Cain kills Abel. The first family is dysfunctional; this should give us all hope! When Cain is asked where Abel is, he lies and says he doesn't know. Lies are ultimately us saying that we don't like the reality we find ourselves in: 'This situation isn't the way I want it to be, so I am going to pretend that it is how I want it to be.' In a way, it is about us saying that we don't trust that God is above everything, so we are taking it into our own hands. Later in the chapter, a guy called Lamech tells his wives (yes, plural) that he too has killed someone. He describes the situation to his wives as, 'I have killed a man for wounding me . . . If Cain is avenged seven times, then Lamech seventy-seven times' (Gen. 4:23,24).

Sin enters the world and the sin against Cain is avenged seven times. A little later, Lamech avenges the sin against him far more. Then in Genesis 6:5, God sees that every thought and heart is now given over to evil all of the time. Every passion, every joy, every moment is now given to evil, not most of the time, not some of the time, but all of the time.

The story starts with dust-man and woman, two people in a broken relationship; Cain kills his brother and is avenged seven times and Lamech, on killing somebody, swears to be avenged eleven times more, and not long after the whole earth is living in evil. The *chatta't* is spiralling out of control. There is a danger with stories like this found in the Old Testament that we read them with our twenty-first century eyes and understanding. We read them looking for solid facts to prove that they happened, but this is not the point. What we need to be asking isn't 'Did this really happen?' but 'What does the story mean?'

The story is about a growing human awareness that everything could fall apart at any moment. We are barely hanging on here. Things are spiralling out of control and there is no way we can stop it. Relationships are full of distrust, people are killing people for revenge, people are killing people for no reason at all. Have you ever had the sense that things are falling apart? That society is imploding in on itself and that the human movement isn't towards love but towards violence, cruelty and deceit?

New technology: The brick

In Genesis 11, we then read a story about how people created the brick. It might sound silly but the brick at one point in history was actually technology. These people decided to build themselves a city with a tower all the way up to the heavens, reaching to God himself. They thought that using their technology they could cut out the need for God and that they could get to the afterlife without needing the Creator. The story goes that they did all of this because they wanted to become famous. People wanted to build stuff, not to help the human race, not to make people's lives better, but because they wanted to make a name for themselves. Fame and being famous was a part of humanity's desire to put itself first, to become powerful. Within eleven chapters of the first book of the Bible, we have people desiring to be known for their grandeur and not because they wanted to help people, support people or care for people. Their sin was to put themselves first, others were less important, others had become people who look up to them and think they're amazing. *Chatta't* had warped their view of themselves. This is a story about technology in the wrong hands.

The story gets us to ask, 'What does sin have to do with me? Do I play any part in this forward movement of violence, broken relationships, pride? Am I continuing the forward rhythm of *chatta't* spiralling out of control? Do I enter into the movement that pushes me forwards so others are held back?' Sin is the human desire for my safety, my rights, my desires, my wants, my power, my glory, me being first, me being more important than every human being and, ultimately, God.

Sin is about us thinking we are more important than God and his movement towards true freedom.

Thinking deeper

- What does sin have to do with you? What is your real feeling towards your behaviour?
- Have you ever felt like you were barely hanging on? What did you find as an encouragement? What supported you, what loved you back to life? Was the local church involved in this process?
- What people group do you see the church is locking out? Do you see the church having any systems of racism, sexism or hatred?
- If *chatta't* separates us from love, then when have you been separated from loving the broken because of your personal attitudes and desires?
- How do you feel, knowing that you have let the broken down because of your own selfish passions?
- Examine yourself for a moment. Reflect on how you have been a part of the forward movement of violence, broken relationships and pride. Now think about the times when you been a part of the movement of love and reconciliation. What brings you greater pleasure? Which brings you life?
- Remember the positive times! Why not write down a list of times you have been a part of rebuilding and reconciling relationships?

Example of resurrection: Two

A real-life story about a person named Sarah:

I was brought up in a loving Christian family who always supported me and never treated me poorly. As long as I can remember, though, I never liked myself; not just a mild dislike, but a full-on loathing. I put this hatred of myself down to the fact that I was bullied through most of my first and middle school; it really got to me.

By high school, things had escalated and this was about the time I started going to a local church. At this church I started to work through with God some of this pain I felt. I would turn up every week and start crying the moment the worship started and generally not stop crying till the meeting had finished. By the end of Year 9, though, I didn't want to do this any more, although I was really feeling close to God, and although I knew that I had to work through this rubbish inside me with him. But I just didn't want to do it any more, it was too painful. So instead of turning to God, I turned away from him and ran as far as I could, looking for other ways to stop myself feeling so hurt.

I started dating guys when I was 15. I never picked nice guys to date, though. I started to date the guys that I thought I deserved to date and, more often than not, these guys were really not good for me. It wasn't their fault; I just disliked myself and my choice in guys showed this. I was just trying to feel something apart from the dislike I had for myself, I just wanted to feel loved and beautiful, and I thought dating these guys would make me feel like that.

When I was 16, however, I went a step further than this. I used to have a female Internet friend who I'd met in a chat room and she told me one day that she was in love with me, which really took me by surprise. The more I thought about it, though, the more the idea appealed to me, and I told this girl I liked her back. Throughout high school I had questioned myself a bit as to whether I liked girls; there were rumours going around that I did, and although I always told people they were rubbish, they made me think. So I started out in what was the most painful and destructive relationship of my life. This girl was just all bad for me. She disliked herself too, and the relationship was just terrible. Every day she would either break up with me or she would tell me she was going to commit suicide and I would spend hours and hours on the phone trying to convince her not to.

All of this happened at the same time as my exams. The painful relationship, my self-hatred and all the pressure I was feeling just got too much for me and I had a breakdown. I was self-harming, I couldn't sleep at night and I became afraid to leave my house every day – irritating, as I had to go out and sit my exams!

Throughout this I could still feel God, I had this huge yearning for him inside of me. I knew that what I was doing wasn't from him; I knew that he wanted me to come to him, to lay it all down before him. But I couldn't.

Eventually I told my parents what was going on with me, how I felt about myself, and my self-harming. Through this I ended up in counselling, and amazingly my counsellor was a Christian. We'd sit every week and go through what was happening in my head, why I was so desperate for love that I would pick people who treated me so badly.

Throughout all of this I was still going to church on and off. It was hard and I didn't really want to be there. I would stand at the back and not really participate in the worship or talk, but I knew that I just had to be there for some reason.

I was in my late teens and had been in counselling for six months when I started to come to some big realizations. I realized that what I was doing to myself wasn't just wrong, it was ripping me apart and killing me inside. I realized that I had to give everything up to God, I needed to hand him all the mess I had caused, and the damage that others had done to me.

One very memorable Sunday this really hit me; by this point, me and my girlfriend had really drifted and we spent more time broken up than together. In the middle of the worship at church I got down on my knees and cried before God, apologizing over and over for how I had run away from him. I told God that I didn't want to feel this way about girls any more, I didn't want to look at girls in the same way and I didn't want to be attracted to them. I asked him to take all this away.

As I knelt, I felt power come over me that I hadn't ever experienced before. In my mind I thought about Jesus' death for me, but then Jesus reminded me of his resurrection. The tomb was empty and Jesus was alive and now his resurrection power was working in me, deep down in my gut.

Something changed in me that night. God started to mould me into the person he wanted me to be; I made the decision to sort out by sexuality and I stopped self-harming.

Since that night, I haven't looked at girls in the same way. I no longer have a single gay impulse. I know that this is only possible because God knew how destructive this was and how it was wrecking my relationship with him.

As for my hate for myself, this was something that took longer. God was there with me, though; I could sleep again and I was no longer afraid to leave the house.

After that Sunday, I continued to go to church. I even worked at the church on a year out. I can't say that I immediately stopped loathing myself, but God started showing me how precious I was to him. He would give others words for me or would speak words of love directly to me. These just broke my heart; they started to make all the pain and hurt melt away. I knew that through God I was loved, that he loved me in a way that no guy or girl ever could, and that only if I loved myself would I ever be able to find real love. It's still not always easy, it's still tempting to start trying to find love that's not from God and see myself as not attractive.

God is the God who wants to hold on to us when we are hurt, to take away the pain, to make life bearable again. But he is more than this: God is the God who wants to totally put us back together again, and I found this in Jesus. The power of Jesus' resurrection can change your life and make you whole again.

The power of his resurrection can comfort and fulfil you in ways that no person or thing can.

3.

The Day that Changed the World

Even if your sins were as great in number as all mankind's put together, still he would not count them against you and he would still have as much confidence in you as he ever had in any creature. If only he finds you ready, he will pay no attention to what you were before. God is God of the present; as he finds a man, so he takes him and accepts him, not for what he has been but for what he is now. All the evil and outrage done to God in sin, he will gladly suffer and suffer for many years to come, if only he may bring man to a better knowledge of his love and make man's affection and thankfulness warmer, his struggle more passionate – as so often it is, after one has sinned.

Meister Eckhart: A Modern Translation
(trans. Raymond Blakney; New York:
Harper and Brothers, 1941), p. 18.

And I was bored

I was 14 and I fell asleep during the Easter Day service. What was awkward was that I was sat in the front row of the church and my head had drooped right down. It wasn't the kind of 'eyes closed' that makes you look like one of those spiritual people who sit there deeply involved in the preaching even though they have eyes shut. This was an obvious and horrific nap pose.

I was snoozing while the preacher spoke about the Easter Day story!

I have sat through many Easter services with that flat feeling of disappointment. Easter Day feels like every other – that feeling you get when it's your birthday and you have to go to work: 'This day is no different to any other; the only difference is I am at church for this.'

A bit about the Mac expert

I recently got myself a new MacBook. My feeling was that if I was going to write another book then I could invest in the thing that was going to help me write it. So I got myself a Macintosh laptop and was amazed at what it could do. I was sat in the church office working on the computer when a colleague from across the room said, 'Why are you doing it like that?' and shouted out a short cut using a function key. This guy knows everything about how a MacBook works, he's even asked if he can start a tip of the day to train the rest of us how to use our computers. He has a much bigger perspective on how brilliant this machine is. I am happy with the computer but have no idea about how much it can do; I am oblivious to its true potential, and this frustrates my colleague. He wants me to see how much it can do and how easy it can make my life.

Often, what the church sells us about the Easter story is a little like the MacBook and me – it's just one corner of its true potential. We go home after being told about this God who dies for us feeling like it somehow doesn't scratch our itch, that this event somehow doesn't change our Monday mornings, or how we walk down the street. Have you ever felt like there has to be more to this?

If I'm honest, for a long time my life felt like a whole string of disappointments. Events went wrong in my life and the Easter story didn't seem to make much of a difference. In this next chapter I want to start to unpack the death and resurrection of Jesus so that we can see that it is much bigger than simply forgiveness of sins, much bigger than a sin management system.

There is a rhythm to history; there are key events that happen after which things change. Somehow life is different because of that event; things can't be the same again. These events are called pivotal events in history.

Caesar, the cross and the phone

I was recently given a book called *Days that Changed the World*. I was hoping it would be a book about ordinary people. Here is Deirdre collecting her kids from school, Steve decorating the bathroom and Patrick doing the cleaning . . . I like stories about real people who do real things, but this wasn't that kind of book. This was a 205-page book looking at fifty world-changing events.

The book is about men and women who have stood at crossroads and have made decisions that have changed the course of world history. The first entry is 15 March 44 BC, 'The Assassination of Julius Caesar' and the second is Good Friday AD 30, 'The Crucifixion of Jesus Christ'. The book starts with the death of the God who created everything and then, very close to the last page, it finishes with 16 October 1973, 'The Rise of Oil Prices'. Jesus and his death are put on a par with oil prices.

It is also put on a par with 7 March 1876 'Alexander Graham Bell Develops the Telephone'.

The death of God the Son on a par with the invention of the phone?

15 August 1945 was the end of the Second World War. From this moment on, millions have agreed that war is not the way forward and there is a growing sense that a new way of peace must be found, and that these wars need to be remembered for our future generations' sake.

20 July 1969 was the day humankind first landed on the moon. From this point on, space was something to be explored, but our place in the universe understood to be so small compared to everything around us. Space is the final frontier and we have started to investigate it. This event sent out a message to the world that the human race can do anything we put our mind to.

9 November 1989, the Berlin Wall came down. This wall was a physical barrier separating West Berlin from the German Democratic Republic/East Germany. The East German government had issued shooting orders to border guards dealing with those trying to climb the wall and cross the border. At least one hundred and thirty-five people were confirmed killed trying to cross the wall into West Berlin before it came down. On 9 November 1989, after several weeks of civil unrest, the East German government announced that all East German citizens could visit West Germany and West Berlin. Crowds of East Germans climbed onto and crossed the wall, joined by West Germans on the other side. The event was a beautiful sight as people received freedom after years of oppression, some having not seen family on the other side for decades. Over the next few weeks, parts of the Berlin Wall were taken down by an excited – and free – public.

For my parent's generation, freedom wasn't a given; people understood that the world was still a messed up place as the freedom of the people of Germany played out on every TV across the world. People who were free realized that freedom wasn't to be taken for granted.

The idea of the World Wide Web has been around since comic books in the 1940s, and in the early seventies a file transfer system through cables was being used; however, it wasn't until years later in 1994 that Netscape was released, allowing the public to use the web. The web has revolutionized the world, allowing communication beyond anything people could have imagined. People are now able to live two lives – one in the real world and one in the cyber world.

11 September 2001 is a date in most of our memories: 9/11 saw nineteen terrorists hijack four planes crashing two into the World Trade Center towers in New York, and one into the Pentagon. The fourth plane crashed into a field near Shanksville in rural Somerset County, Pennsylvania, after some of its passengers and flight crew attempted to retake control of the plane. Not counting the nineteen hijackers, 2,974 people died in the attacks and another twenty-four have never been found, presumed dead. The events of 9/11 have left the world feeling unsure of its safety and more aware of global issues. More of us now know more about the Middle East, and how the West is viewed there. We have shown far more interest in Islam, many of us trying to understand if we in the West played a part in these events because of our behaviour.

The world hasn't been the same since the Second World War, neither has it been the same since every home has been able to surf the net. Both these events have changed our nation and have changed the way we live out our lives, for better or worse. *All* the events above have played their part in how the world has changed. But they only have future implications, the world is only changed post the event; the days, weeks and years before the event don't change in light of the event.

A bigger event

But what if there was an event that not only had future implications but also changed and restored the past? What if there was an event that changed the way we see everything before that event, and ultimately redefines it and restores it?

The cross has become an event stuck in time, which has a specific religious significance. This is why it can be placed in a book of fifty world-changing events. What if this event had no religious significance at all but had a raw, daily, dirt-of-the-ground kind of significance? What if this event had nothing to do with religion and had everything to do with the reality of life? The day to day treadmill of Monday mornings was affected in some way by this event and not just the one hour on a Sunday? I would like to argue that the cross of Christ and his resurrection transcends and stands apart from all other historical events, not because this is a religious event but because everything finds its proper place in it.

A letter to a city

Paul in AD 60 decided to write a letter to the people of Colossae setting out who Jesus was and what he did on the cross. Paul had to write this letter because they hadn't fully grasped the true depth of who this Christ was, and heretics had come into the city and confused people even further. Colossae had been a prosperous textile and wool industry. It was well populated and had become large and wealthy. The wool that Colossae had produced was dark red and was known as colossinium wool. Because of the city's wealth and work, it had brought in many Jewish and Phrygian trade and workers. When these workers arrived, they brought with them their own philosophies and religions and this had created a city with a mixture of religious ideas and thoughts. The people here were happy to create a 'pick 'n' mix' religion made from lots of different faiths and ideologies from all over the known world. The content of Paul's letter reflects the fact that Colossae was a city with a mixture of religious ideas, political thoughts and social concepts with the people into bits of everything. I'm so glad we don't live in a world like this, aren't you?

Paul's focus isn't on sin or the law but instead on the culture, with an emphasis on the unique claims of Jesus, not merely one of a long list of gods but the one true God who redefined everything. Culture had influenced the church and Paul wanted to stamp out all confusion about Christ and his death.

Paul writes in Colossians 1:18–20:

> He [Jesus] was supreme in the beginning and—leading the resurrection parade—he is supreme in the end. From beginning to end he's there, towering far above everything, everyone. So spacious is he, so roomy, that everything of God finds its proper place in him without crowding. Not only that, but all the broken and dislocated pieces of the universe—people and things, animals and atoms—get properly fixed and fit together in vibrant harmonies, all because of his death, his blood that poured down from the cross.

> *(The Message)*

Standing above

The church had started to place Christ's death in a timeline, giving it a date and a place. But this event stands above all other events; it towers above, looking down on all other world history. This event is the event through which Paul welcomes us to reread all world history; as though Jesus' death and resurrection is made of glass and through it we are able to see the past and the future. It is impossible to see the cross without seeing world history, and it is impossible to see world history without seeing the cross. World history, no matter who you are, if you believe in it or not, can only be understood in Jesus.

Paul writes that Jesus, in his resurrection state, towers above everything and everyone, being so spacious that everything finds its proper place in him. All world history finds its place within Jesus' death and resurrection. It's not that these events didn't happen, but it's that through Jesus and his resurrection that he has welcomed all of the broken and damaged fragments back together in harmony.

The Message translation then defines what these broken things are: 'Not only that, but all the broken and dislo-cated pieces of the universe—people and things, animals and atoms—get properly fixed' (Col. 1:18).

People are changed because of Jesus' resurrection.

The kettle is changed because of Jesus' resurrection.

The bunny is changed because of Jesus' resurrection.

Even the atom is changed because of Jesus' resurrection. People, objects, bunnies and dirt all come back to their proper place because of what Jesus did on the cross.

More than sin management

Too long has the cross been about a sin management system, like a car wash for the soul. But what if the whole system is screwed and nothing is running as it should, the whole system needs rebuilding and repairing? Jesus' death is not just a machine to deal with our sin, but stands above the whole of history as the redeeming event within which the whole of the created order finds its proper place. This is big stuff. The world could never be the same after the day Jesus rose from the dead. Surely the sun shone a little brighter that morning; maybe the bunny hopped higher and had a glint in its eye; maybe the atom, the building block of the universe, was pulled kicking and screaming back into proper relationship with God.

Paul then says that because of Christ everything is brought back to vibrant harmony because of his blood. Vibrant harmony? The actual word here originates from the Hebrew word *shalom* which we badly translate as peace.

Shalom is one of those words that holds many angles and concepts within it. It means a state of perfection, a place of being whole; it's about being connected and integrated, it's about blessing, completeness and something being res-tored to a beautiful original state. This concept of being connected and integrated is about God, ourselves, others and all of creation working and joining in harmony and relationship. Jesus' death and resurrection brings *shalom* to all things: God, ourselves, others and creation.

We don't quite know what to do with *shalom* so we simply render it as peace. One rabbi described *shalom* as being so marinated and soaked in grace and blessing that you can't help being transformed.

All the broken pieces of the universe – the woman who's just lost her baby, the family who's struggling to support an addicted son, the kettle that doesn't boil, and the atom – get properly fixed and fit together in *shalom* with God, vibrant harmony. All because of Jesus' death and resurrection.

He has things worked out and it's not all about us

Paul earlier in Colossians writes, '. . . all things were created by him and for him. He is before all things, and in him all things hold together' (Col. 1:16,17). In Jesus everything holds together. God does not change the circumstances of our lives, neither did God change Jesus' circumstances on the cross. But Jesus' death and resurrection is proof that God's purpose and plan for this world is stronger than everything else, and it will triumph because Jesus is the one holding it all together.

There is a cross standing over history and it is proof that God has everything worked out. Billy Graham, the American evangelist, once said that 'the entire plan for the future [of the world] has its key in the resurrection [of Jesus]'. If we simply make Jesus' death and resurrection into this sin management system then we ignore the deeper truth that it is not all about us. We still have a problem in that we human beings think everything is to do with us, as if we are the only important element of the whole created order. Jesus comes for all things.

Paul, writing to the Philippians again makes the point by saying that Jesus 'who will transform these humble bodies of ours into the likeness of his glorious body by means of that power by which he is able to subject [rebuild or restore] *all things* to himself' (Phil. 3:21, NET, emphasis mine).

The Greek word used by Paul for 'all things' is the word *panta*, which means entire, whole, total. It is translated in other sections as all the earth, or the entire creation; other translators try to unpack its depth by saying every element of God's created order, nothing is left out of this, everything is counted as in.

Rogue Lego bricks

My son has a large yellow box of Lego; it's the kind of box that holds a ridiculous amount and it's a boys dream. You can build almost anything with this amount of bricks. Recently Isaac has taken to building bigger and bigger projects, and on this occasion he was building the monster of all castles. The problem was he needed every brick. He was taking other Lego creations and breaking them down so they could be part of this new project, the monster of all projects. He was running around looking for rogue bricks that could be in this giant castle. Isaac was searching out every last brick that had been left on the sofa, in the kitchen, because he wanted this to be the biggest and best building project he had ever been involved in. We were even looking behind the fridge. Everything was in, nothing was left out.

God so valued his creation that he wanted everything to be in, everything to be used for the restoring of the world, nothing was left out. God has a monster of a restoration plan and not even the atom could be left out.

There is a great story that Jesus tells in Matthew 18. It's the story of a shepherd who has 100 sheep but one goes missing. The shepherd searches out that one lost sheep, because every one of these sheep were important and were needed, nothing could be lost because the flock were all worth it. When the shepherd finds his lost sheep he celebrates and parties, inviting all his friends and neighbours round. We're happy to apply this story to us, saying God loves us all, but isn't it interesting that we never see the story wider than ourselves? God's heart is for all his creation; no brick is left out, no atom is left hidden behind the fridge.

It is important to remember that things are redeemed but, at this time, still not perfect. We live in a world where we are still waiting to see the full restoration. It's like Holy Saturday; the disciples had seen their Jesus die and were waiting for resurrection to happen. Sunday was coming, but they were still stuck in Saturday. We have the knowledge that resurrection has happened, but we sit waiting for Sunday to come.

Thinking deeper

Colossians 1:18–20 (*The Message*):

He [Jesus] was supreme in the beginning and—leading the resurrection parade—he is supreme in the end. From beginning to
end he's there, towering far above everything, everyone. So
spacious is he, so roomy, that everything of God finds its proper place in him without crowding. Not only that, but all the broken and dislocated pieces of the universe—people and things,
animals and atoms—get properly fixed and fit together in
vibrant harmonies, all because of his death, his blood that
poured down from the cross.

- In this reading Jesus is described as 'So spacious . . . [and]
  roomy'. What does this mean to you? What does it mean
  for your shortcomings and baggage? What does it mean
  for the things that have been said or done to you? Is the
  Jesus you know this big?
- Paul then says that because of Christ everything is
  brought back to vibrant harmony because of his blood.
  Vibrant harmony? When have you seen this practised
  around you? Have you experienced a moment when you
  glimpsed what this vibrant harmony looked like?
- Some people have put the death of God the Son on a par
  with the invention of the phone. They see Jesus as just
  another historical event. How would you say you see the
  death and resurrection of God the Son? Merely history or
  something bigger?

- If you were to speak to someone who had never heard of Jesus, how would you describe the cross event? Would it be that of a sin management system, or would you have a better and bigger way of helping someone understand this event?
- How have you experienced the bigness of the cross in your own life?
- How have you practised this big story in the lives of the broken around you? Has it been by action, words or something else?

Example of resurrection: Three

A real-life story about a person named Dom

I grew up living with my mum and never really saw my dad. They had split up before I even hit one. Jesus and the church to me were always this alien group who never had any impact on the reality of life.

When I was a young teen, we moved to the outskirts of London where I got to know a group of young people who seemed really nice. They were interested in me and they never imposed their views on me. They sometimes invited me to gigs and parties and they were fun to be around. Then one day I realized that some of this group were Christians and that they attended church regularly. I couldn't understand why they would go to such a thing. I started to chat with them about what they believed, and the Jesus they spoke about wasn't the weak Jesus I had heard about at school or in the media.

This Jesus seemed to be interested in me – not just in having me as a member of his society, but really wanting to see my life lived a better way. I realized that this group believed that Jesus worked in people's lives for good every day and not just on a Sunday at their holy services.

Over a period of time, I chatted with one friend in particular who also turned out to be new to this Jesus thing. He had started to attend church a year before, and he spoke of the others in the group as loving people who wanted to help sort out the mess of his life.

This group never seemed to criticize me or judge me but wanted to get to know me. I noticed that over the six months I had been hanging out with them they had helped me see my life in a very different way. I had always wanted to blame people for my family not being a 'normal' family (whatever that is). I had also been angry at us moving home and leaving old friends behind, but now I started to see that it wasn't worth being angry at what had happened but that I could find new meaning in this guy called Jesus.

I started to attend this church with my friends thinking they were going to ask me to sign up to lots of things and commit to become a religious nutter. It was weird, they didn't, they just invited me to realize I wasn't the person God had originally created me to be and that events in my life had made me see myself and family in a distorted way. During the first few months attitudes I didn't even know I had came to the surface. I never saw myself as sexist, but I noticed that my attitude to women changed; I wasn't as rude and stopped telling jokes that were anti-women. I also realized I didn't always tell the whole truth, or distorted the truth to make myself look better; I now didn't feel like I needed to do that.

It wasn't this group of people who did any of this, it was Jesus who each day was transforming me, making me more like the kind of guy he was. I'm becoming less critical and choose to not enter into talking about others as much. I want to see others come to realize that Jesus' resurrection isn't there to condemn us or make us religious, but to give us a new hope, a new life.

I had always seen Jesus as someone who was telling me off, but he isn't, he's the God who welcomes us to join in all things being made new, and it started with me. Now I have joined in this movement that wants others to see people being made new and whole. I have also realized that my whole life is about passing this resurrection life on, not just to people but also to creation. I have started to recycle paper, plastics, clothes, and I have chosen to wear less new clothes and keep wearing old clothes till they wear out. For me, it's about me passing this life on to the whole of creation. My whole life should allow resurrection life to flow from it.

I think I have only just started to understand what this means for me, but I am so excited to see where it goes.

4.

Born to Die – True Raw Power

He sees through bleary eyes.
He touches and feels with bloodied hands.
He stumbles and falls on rough sands, sharp stones.
Roman hands guide him to his feet.
He has his burden taken from him.
He walks with faltering feet.
Up to the hill.

Humiliated, humbled by those he has created.
Nails plunge deep, breaking flesh.
He cries through cracked lips.
He breathes with laboured lungs.
He paints his blood on the doorposts of the universe,

as he dies to liberate the world.

'His Death' by Jared Lovell (2009)

Victims of real power

It was Sunday morning and even the sun was shining a little brighter; something had changed, something was new about this day. Mary Magdalene and other women made their way down to the tomb where Jesus had been placed two days before. This was their first chance to prepare him for the tomb and, as they arrived, they found that the large stone blocking the entrance had been rolled away. Imagine their anger that someone had stolen the body – or maybe the Roman Empire had planned to take it. When they entered there was no Jesus, just a pile of used grave clothes. Turning around, the women saw two men standing at the entrance dressed in bright shining clothes. One of the men spoke and said, 'Why do you look for the living among the dead? He is not here; he has risen' (Luke 24:5,6).

Jesus dies receiving the best the empire could throw at him, taking their violence, their punishment, and flips it around so that it becomes an event that ultimately destroys evil.

The Roman Empire's assumption was that by killing Jesus they would make him the victim of the empire, and that by doing this they would take away his power, and that the whole movement was over. They thought it would be a clean death and the followers would go home and it was all done and dusted. How wrong could they have been? By executing Jesus, his resurrection had made the empire the victim of the true authority and power. Jesus had taken on the whole system of the empire which had believed that it had won because he had died at their hands. Jesus showed them who was the most powerful by raising himself above death itself. Jesus was never the victim of the empire. The empire was the victim of Jesus' true power. We assume that the one with the strongest fist is in fact the strongest, but Jesus showed how true power uses others' power to make it yours.

There was nothing worse they could have done to him, and now the man in the bright shiny dress is saying, 'He has risen!' *Jesus is alive!*

Imagine how it felt for the Early Church to say the slogan 'Jesus is alive'. Their rabbi had died, they had seen it happen, and now Jesus was really alive, walking and talking with his followers. It probably felt amazing, fantastic, and breathtaking to say. I recently watched the 2008 American election on TV, and on the night Barack Obama won the vote, people were chanting 'Obama, Obama, Obama' as though it was some kind of mantra, over and over like the name Obama itself held life, and gave them life to say.

Imagine the early followers sitting days after the event saying over and over, 'Jesus is alive!', almost like the words gave life to their disbelief.

As we have looked at over the last few chapters, Jesus' resurrection is much bigger than simply a tool to destroy our own personal sin. It's a much deeper event.

To show what it looked like

Jesus was born to show the world what it looked like to live out a life totally connected to God and he was born for the purpose of his death.

Did you know that you and I are also born to die? It wasn't just Jesus who was selected to die for us, but that Jesus now invites us to die too. When I say this I don't mean to die of old age or of a horrid illness. Jesus has called us to die, today, right now.

Jesus came as the perfect sacrifice to set us free from our *chatta't*. But Jesus wants us to be more than just free from sin, he wants us to join him in letting our own lives go. At one point, Jesus turns to a crowd that are following him and speaks clearly about what he wants his followers to do. Jesus says, 'If anyone would come after me, he must deny himself and take up his cross and follow me' (Mark 8:34).

But what does Jesus actually mean when he says we need to take up our cross and follow him? If we take up our cross and follow Jesus, where are we going, exactly?

On the day of someone's crucifixion, the person would carry the cross to where? They would carry it to the place of their death. Jesus is inviting those listening to pick up their cross and agree to follow him to their death. This isn't a literal cross and a literal physical death Jesus is talking about, it is a much more exciting death than that.

Jesus is inviting us to die to ourselves, to let our own plans die, let our own selfish desires die, our own pride die, our own empires die, and to leave it all to follow him.

Letting it die

This death is about making ourselves less important, about not taking ourselves too seriously, not seeking to make ourselves look like the most important person in the room. It's about letting the part of us that is about our ego, our pride, and our *chatta't* die; to not go back there and entertain that part of us any more. Jesus invites us to die with him, giving ourselves over to the redemption of all things, being his workers. It's about joining in Jesus' movement, being given a tool kit and being Jesus' hands and feet in the world.

We were born to die, born to let ourselves go in order that Jesus might be resurrected in us. Jesus then resurrected in us works through us to resurrect others. This is why it's so important to be surrounded by other resurrected people, surrounded by others who are dying to themselves and giving life because of Jesus. To be a part of this community means if you are struggling, doubting, feeling unable to carry on, this group of resurrected beings should bring you life as they have life flow from them.

So often, followers of Jesus simply see themselves as for-given and then wait to find out what happens next, as if there is going to be something else done to them, and all along don't realize that they are still holding onto their own lives. Jesus is looking for people who will put everything in, holding nothing back, so that they can become reborn, resurrected in Jesus.

Didn't hear that one preached

There's an utterly brilliant story in the Bible, found in the book of Acts. It's the kind of story the church avoids preaching on because it looks so odd some people might be confused by it. Jesus had sent out his followers to build this resurrection com-munity, a community of people dying to themselves to bring life to others; they had been filled with this life-giving Spirit and now were getting on with the task of starting this church. People were committing to it and were even giving all they had to the common purse. They were placing their monthly earn-ings into one central pot, and then from this pot they gave back to people what they needed, and what was left over they used to work with the poor. It was a mass feeding programme paid for by the church; some would describe this as a resurrection project: people giving up their own right to what they have earned so that others might have life.

The story goes that people were selling their land and devoting it to this Jesus movement. Giving everything away, knowing that when they needed financial help they could then turn to the church. Many of the people giving up their land for sale were actually selling their inheritance, these fields were the fall-back plan if life got hard. It wasn't like they had a pen-sion plan that would come up for renewal when they hit 65; they needed a way of paying for life when they got old and their fields were it.

Nevertheless, people were committing everything to this resurrection community and many more were joining. In Acts 5, a couple called Ananias and Sapphira had said that they, too, wanted to give their pension plan to the church; they said they would sell their land and give it to the church for the common pot. But they changed their minds and decided not to give everything to the church but keep a little back, just in case. Rather than committing their whole lives, they decided to keep a small percentage in a Jerusalem bank to draw upon if this movement fell apart. The problem was that they didn't tell any-one that this was what they were doing – they lied and said they were giving everything. Peter knew that they were holding something back and consequently both of them were killed by God. Quite an odd story really. The reality was that the Jewish movement had been full of hypocrites in the past that had said they were doing one thing for God and did another; people who didn't totally commit to God's movement in the world.

God needed to send a warning shot to the church that hypocrisy was not a part of this new resurrection community. This resurrection community was about giving everything to Jesus, it was about dying to self so that Jesus could be resur-rected in us, and this could not happen if we chose to hold areas of our lives back. It was an 'all or nothing' response Jesus wanted.

Murder, fish food and repentance

There are lots of examples of people dying to self to be resur-rection within the Bible. One such example is Jonah. Jonah was a proud man who hated his neighbours in Nineveh. This story was one of those that I grew up hearing in Sunday school. It's a strange story really, not the kind of story you really want to tell children. It's the story of a man being thrown off the side of a boat and then eaten alive by a large fish.

Jonah being told by God to go and tell Nineveh to repent causes Jonah to run away from God and the city of Nineveh. To understand Jonah's response it is important that we first understand the city he wants to run away from.

Nineveh was the capital of the Assyrian Empire and was found in what's now northern Iraq. The name Nineveh is an Assyrian translation of an early name for the goddess Ishtar, the goddess of fertility, love and war. Her cult practises involved sacred prostitution with the hope that this sex worship would stimulate the other gods to mate and create, thus earning Ishtar the title 'courtesan of the gods'.

Ishtar appears on wall hangings, seals and paintings of the period as a mighty warrior who fights for and defends her people and king by crippling her opponents in battle. King Ashurbanipal who reigned after Jonah in 669–631 BC was described as crying before the goddess like an infant asking his mother for help. Ishtar's power and might as a divine warrior is depicted on carvings by having weapons rising from her shoulders, arms and even legs.

Nineveh was a beautiful city with wide boulevards, large squares, parks and gardens and prided itself on its art, sculptures and wall carvings, very much like our world capitals today. It was typical of most Assyrian cities with fifteen large gates all named after deities. The Assyrians were noted for their vast knowledge of warfare and organization, with an unwillingness to lose in battle. At the height of its wealth and power, Nineveh was enclosed by an inner wall 12 km long, wide enough to ride three chariots around side by side. With a population of 120,000 people it was also the largest settlement worldwide at the time. Nineveh was powerful, it crippled all those who stood in its way and was known for its *chatta't* behaviour. This wasn't the kind of place a nice Jewish boy would want to know.

Nineveh's wealth and military power, combined with a flair for battle, made them unconquerable and therefore much feared by people like Jonah. Since they were generally considered unconquerable most wanted to ally with them; better to be the friend of the enemy than challenge them. Some have described them as a 'psychotic Assyrian battlefront'. There is no surprise that Jonah was afraid to go and challenge them, even in the name of YHVH.

He feared death and imprisonment with a message that said, 'Go to the great city of Nineveh and preach against it, because its wickedness has come up before me' (Jonah 1:2). Jonah's fear was genuine and understandable. Jonah didn't want to go, not only because he feared for his life, but also because he had a racist hate for them. Those people of Nineveh were evil in the sight of Jonah and his people. People would walk miles around the area just to miss out Nineveh on their journey.

Jonah jumps on a ship and tries to run to Tarshish. This is a story about God wanting Jonah to die to his own personal hate for a group of people, and to go and speak resurrection life to Nineveh. Jonah was not willing to die to set this city free.

How often do we do this? How often do we run away from people we need to speak life to, all because we aren't willing to die to our own pride, or aren't willing to die to our hate?

Jonah on the run from Nineveh ends up in the mouth of a giant fish, he ultimately realizes what is happening and, in the belly of the fish, calls out to God. Jonah is now willing to allow himself to die, giving up all pride, all hate, all contempt for this group of people God is wanting to bring back to life. Jonah gets spat out on the beach and walks to the city of Nineveh. The story ends with the city realizing their *chatta't* and receiving resurrection life.

This story is about that story

Often stories in the Bible are pointers to other stories – this story is actually about that story. Often the Jonah story is spoken about as a pointer to Jesus because Jonah was in the belly of the fish for three days. But this story is much bigger than that; maybe this story can only be understood in light of Jesus' resurrection story. Now, in Jesus this story makes sense. It's the story of a human being called by God to speak resurrection to a city that is utterly messed up. Jonah, unwilling to allow his own hate and pride to die, runs away in the opposite direction. This story is about us, and how if we aren't willing to let our own pride and hate die, then we end up like Jonah, running in the opposite direction.

This Jesus movement found in Acts wants people to give every small and dark bit of our lives so that we might be 'resurrection life' to the people and places like Nineveh.

> Swapping:
> Bitterness for forgiveness;
> Pride for humility;
> Addiction for freedom;
> Gossip for fact;
> Ignorance for awareness;
> Control for autonomy;
> Blindness for openness;
> Lies for honesty;
> Shame for self-respect;
> Ego for others;
> Arrogance for meekness;
> Fashion for contentment;
> TV for reality.

We all have things to leave so that we might die to self, to gain real life in Jesus. Let's for a moment think practic-ally what this would look like if we did. For an example, what would this look like on our next birthday? What kind of things would we wish people would give us as gifts? What might be on the birthday list?

A new mobile?
Money for some new clothes?
Tickets to see a band or play?
A DVD box set?
Jewellery?
Some strange gadget?
iPod?
A guitar?
A piano?
A party?
Gift vouchers?
A laptop?

All these are good things, but if we're dying and Jesus is resurrecting us, what would Jesus want us to have for our birthday?

Over the last few years as I have been dying so that Jesus would be resurrecting me, I have noticed that I have been less interested in the world's upward spiral of acquiring more stuff. I have been increasingly happy living with less.

Affluenza is killing us

It has been obvious to doctors and sociologists in the last two decades that more and more people are becoming ill with depression, anxiety, tiredness, being lethargic and other things that affect people's positive outlook on life. Previously we have put depression and anxiety down as a medical illness, but Affluenza is an illness that people are increasingly becoming aware of, and at the same time realizing that so many people don't even know they have it. Affluenza is a term that critics of consumerism have used to express what is happening all over the West. If I were to create a dictionary definition of this it would be something like:

Affluenza is the bloated, lethargic and discontented feeling that results from need to keep up with 'the Joneses'. Stemming from the stress of trying to be someone, prove yourself, have the next new thing and live the dream life, it is the unsustainable addiction to economic growth, resulting in the compulsion of the pursuit of more things. It is very contagious, easily transmitted and results in anxiety and lack of real happiness.

Life for so many has become one big shopping spree; changing appearance, tastes and hobbies each year to fit with the next fashionable thing. More and more people are claiming that their houses aren't big enough, not for the number of people living in them but because they have so much stuff to store; it is common to hear people say, 'I don't have enough storage.' The average house being built now is a third larger than houses built in the early nineties, which were a third larger than the houses built in the eighties.

Many people are buying the larger car with more features not because they need it but because it says, 'I'm the kind of person that can afford to drive this kind of car.'

Shopping centres or malls have become the centres of community. People meet there to catch up and grab a coffee while doing some idle and spontaneous shopping.

Shopping has become therapy, the place to go to rehab from the mundane life.

The whole system of knowing how we are doing in life has become about comparison. Comparing ourselves to those around us, checking on the league table of success.

More people are attending shopping centres each week than churches, synagogues or mosques. On average, people spend six hours a week shopping and only fifty minutes a week playing with their children (Source: *Youthwork Magazine*, September 2008).

People shop to make them feel better. Feeling like they can become someone with that new item.

Do we own all of our things – homes, cars, MP3 players and DVD collections, the hair straighteners and the designer shoes – or is it that they own us?

Addicted to shopping

I met a woman at a conference recently who was sharing about her addiction to shopping and designer clothes. She has been a Christian for years but had avoided ever talking about her love of all things fashionable. This passion for shopping and clothes had told her that she was beautiful and valued but in reality she never felt content, there had to be something better around the corner that would make her happier. And all along she was going to church worshipping Jesus but still looking for acceptance in fashion. When asked if she would help serve on a mission weekend, her response was 'No, I'm busy that weekend.' The truth was she was busy shopping, not with friends or family, but on her own. It was at this point she realized she needed to die to this addiction; she needed to be set free so that Jesus would bring her real life.

Affluenza tells us that if we buy this new product then we will be loved and accepted, but on the other hand it says that we aren't lovable and accepted without it. We seek self-esteem from the upward spiral of having more and being more important but this leaves us without a genuine sense of identity.

This Affluenza virus isn't anything new and was certainly problematic in Jesus' day. On one occasion we are told that a rich man comes to Jesus asking how he can get eternal life (Matt. 19:16–22). In this encounter, Jesus takes note that the young man is living by the Law, he hasn't murdered, he's not committed adultery, he's not stolen and he's honoured his father and mother. We know that this is a young man who has great wealth; we also know that he has lived by the Law and therefore he's not gained his money from indecent means, the money is not stolen.

This young man has worked hard for his money, it's justifiably his, which means we can presume he has status; his money would have made him someone to be admired, looked up to, someone who has all the right things in life. Jesus recognizes that this young man's problem is that he's a part of this upward rhythm of importance, money and the world of opportunity. Jesus tells him to get rid of it all, to step away from this life, give all his money away and be free.

To die to Affluenza and to be raised in 'eternal life'.

Aionion

The word used for eternal in the Gospels is *aionion*. *Aionion* is a divine and supernatural life with attributes that are powered by a divine force found in life itself. This life is an unending real life, it's undivided and very present. This isn't a life that starts once your pulse stops and you breathe your last, it's a life that starts now. One modern Jewish teacher, Rabbi Daniel Nessim, once said that it was like life on caffeine.

This young man asks, 'How do I get this eternal, undivided real life?' and Jesus says, 'Die to Affluenza, die to the upward rhythm of importance, fame and stuff. Die to your addiction to more, stop hanging onto a thing which falsely defines you.' The young man's response is to walk away miserable because his great wealth is the deep addiction that is holding him back.

He could not do it, he could not let himself die, so he walks away miserable.

Jesus is calling his church to die to this rhythm of the world and follow him. A number of years ago, my wife and I decided that we just didn't need two cars, we could live with one, do more walking and use public transport. So we gave the second car away, and we started to live a little lighter. I also decided to stop buying DVDs and use the money more wisely. This isn't to say we are anywhere near perfect, but we are trying. Many of us at church have started to buy less physical gifts and buy more gifts for people that actually benefit those living in poverty. Last year as a family we were given one lamb, a family of pigs and medical jabs for ten children. Doesn't this make us sound great? The reality is we aren't, and we are nowhere near perfect, but we recognize that we need to make a start.

Fake self-esteem

Jesus sees a church dying of Affluenza and asks us to pick up our cross and follow him to a death where we become free from this upward spiral of self-importance, feeling valued by stuff, and gaining a fake self-esteem from the new product.

There is another problem with those who suffer from Affluenza – they think their time is theirs. They say things like 'It is my right to do what I want with my time', or 'I have been so busy working to live that I have no time to help anyone else'. Affluenza falsely tells us that our lives are for our comfort and that we are to work to make our time easier. It also tells us that we deserve our time, we have earned it, we can take and not give back.

Could it be that God wants us to die to the idea that we have any rights to our time? At the end of the day, didn't God give it to us? Our time comes from him. Could it be that God would like us to die to the idea that I can do what I wish with my time, to be resurrected into the idea that my time is given to me to be resurrection life to others?

I spoke to a lady not so long ago who serves every weekend at a homeless shelter near us. She gives her Saturdays freely, unpaid so that she can serve the poor, often neglected by our society.

Could it be that we die to 'our' time to be resurrected into Jesus' time? Serving in feeding programmes, housing programmes, after-school clubs, charity shops, campaigning for human rights?

What part of our lives does Jesus want us to die to so that we might live a full life in another area? What does Jesus want us to sacrifice so that we might bring life to others? Do we really need that new mobile phone, could we live with what we have and choose for our birthdays not to receive, but to give? Isn't it funny that on Jesus' birthday we have gifts given to us and then, on our birthdays, we do the same and have more stuff given to us? Do we need those gift vouchers or could someone we know benefit from them? Do we need more gadgets to fill our houses with, or could we get the gift giver to buy us a pig for a Third World family?

Grain and a jalapeño

I'm not a farmer and I don't claim to be one, so I don't fully understand how one man is able to plant such small seeds and produce so many crops. Farming was a day to day image for those living in the Middle East. Lots of Jesus' teaching was based on his walks around the farming areas of Galilee.

I love a good jalapeño pepper. You can't beat a good spicy pizza or chillies on a burger. A number of years ago when I first started to be creative with food, I cooked a meal for some friends that consisted of chargrilled chillies. On my plate sat a large chargrilled jalapeño and I was so overjoyed to see the red cooked skin that I became overenthusiastic and took a large juicy bite from it.

That next moment was like all hell broke loose. My eyes were crying and my mouth was burning. I drank pints of milk in the hope of trying to dampen down the pain of the taste sensation.

If you haven't ever eaten a good quality chilli, then you have never felt the wonderful hummmmm sensation in your throat and mouth. When you eat a chilli, you know you're alive.

Last year, I decided to try and grow my own chillies. I bought a few from the supermarket and decided to pick out the seeds and sit them in the sun on my window ledge. I don't know much about farming, but I do know a seed needs to die before it can release new growth. The seeds sat there for a number of months and I then potted them up and watched life spring from these dead, dried seeds. Over a period of time, the chilli plants grew, and I saw white flowers bud and then these formed into juicy red chillies.

The whole universe is built upon this rhythm. Something always has to die for something new to be born. When you pick an apple from a tree, from that moment it's in the process of dying. All the food you put on your table is in the process of death, it has been picked from its life source and now provides life to us.

Jesus understood this concept and in John 12:24 tells us that 'unless a grain of wheat falls into the ground and dies, it remains alone; but if it dies, it produces much grain' (NKJV). This is how the whole universe is built, death brings life.

Jesus is saying that unless something dies, fruit cannot be birthed. He is indicating that if our lives do not bring forth fruit, then we have not yet learned to die.

How do we get a huge tree? A seed must die first and be planted.

How do we see someone grow into who they were designed to be? Someone must be willing to die and be life replanted.

Father, forgive them

Jesus, in Luke 23, while hung on the cross, prayed, 'Father, for-give them'. Jesus dying wanted to still see people set free from their hideous behaviour. Yet the only way the Father could for-give them was the very act of Jesus' death: Jesus' crucifixion. Without the shedding of blood, there is no forgiveness of sin.

Jesus' death was the way for a new life to be birthed in the world. It was because of his blood that fell to the dusty ground of the cross; his death brought others back to life. Jesus' prayer was answered in his death.

Could it be that sometimes our prayers might be answered in our death?

Worth dying for

Martin Luther King said life is not worth living unless you find something worth dying for. Isn't the Jesus' resurrection project worth dying for? Isn't this worth giving our lives for?

Many of us live our lives thinking that Jesus died for us and therefore we are free to wait until he returns so that we can enter heaven, and until then we need to work to make our lives cosy and easy. Jesus wasn't the only one born to die, we were too. We are born so that we would die, allowing Jesus to live in us, and that his love, grace and life would be seen through us, through his resurrection in us.

Jesus knew that we would not be happy, we would not be free to live this glorious life until we fully committed our lives to picking up our cross and following him.

The Roman Empire had believed that by killing Jesus they would stop his new way of seeing life, faith and religion. They thought that they could stamp this Jesus movement out and that the whole thing would implode, and within a few years the movement would be over. That's why Jesus' death is so brilliant: Jesus subverts the whole rhythm of the universe, death is no longer final and the fist no longer the way of measuring someone's true power.

After forty days, Jesus tells his followers to take this new resurrection life called the gospel out into the world, out from Jerusalem (the religious) to the ends of the earth (not religious). Jesus' message wasn't now just for those who had read the Torah or previously worshipped at the Temple.

The story goes that the disciples started sharing this message, not just through words but also actions, and that every time the political or religious empire tried to stop it leaving Jerusalem it seemed to fall through their fingers. They started to kill members of this Jesus movement in the hope that this would scare them into stopping, but as they were already dying to themselves there was nothing to be scared of. These resurrection people were becoming more and more passionate about this new movement.

It says that in Acts 2:41 that there were about three thousand added to the number of followers on the day of Pentecost. By Acts 4, the number had grown so much that they could only count the number of men, which was about five thousand, and by Acts 5 all that they could say was 'more and more' people were added. This movement was unable to stop people joining and dying to themselves to allow life to flow through them.

In Acts 5, Peter and the other apostles were arrested for the resurrection work they were doing and were asked to argue their case. After hearing their message one rabbi called rabbi Gamaliel said: 'Judas the Galilean appeared in the days of the census and led a band of people in revolt. He too was killed, and all his followers were scattered. Therefore, in the present case I advise you: Leave these men alone! Let them go! For if their purpose or activity is of human origin, it will fail. But if it is from God, you will not be able to stop these men; you will only find yourselves fighting against God' (Acts 5:37–39).

These followers had found something worth dying for, and it had given them life. Are we dying to ourselves so that we might have life, or are we a church that thinks it's all about Jesus' death?

We need to be willing to give up our own desires so that Jesus' desires might grow in us. Jesus needs his church to be passing on his death, but also passing on ours. The church isn't a bunch of Sunday worshippers longing and waiting for Jesus' return. The church is a resurrection project with Jesus raising people back to life so that they can be life to others. A church that spurs each other on in dying and rising, a church not only dying for Jesus but dying, too, for the world.

Thinking deeper

- Imagine how the Early Church felt to say the slogan 'Jesus is alive'. When have you been a part of a movement that had a slogan so powerful? How would you feel about using this slogan as powerfully as they did – and how would you feel about using it down at the local estate?
- Jesus is inviting you to follow him and die. How does this make you feel? Are you willing for this to happen, or are you apprehensive? Take maybe five to ten minutes to reflect on how this feels. How comfortable are you with this idea?
- What things might Jesus be asking you to allow to die, so that you can allow him to be resurrected in you?
- Where are you heading? Jonah was off on his trip to Tarshish when God wanted him to do mission work in the Middle East. What have you run away from? What have you focused on so that you can successfully negotiate around God's call on your life?
- Answer this question honestly: Do you compare yourself and what you own with what others have?
- In Matthew 19 we meet the rich young man who struggles to give up his wealth to follow Jesus. More people are attending shopping centres each week than churches, synagogues or mosques. On average, people spend six hours a week shopping and only fifty minutes a week playing with their children. How did the section on Affluenza make you feel? Would you be willing to give up everything, even your time spent shopping, to follow Jesus?

Example of resurrection: Four

A real-life story about a person named Becky:

I grew up in a dysfunctional family with my mum, stepdad and a couple of brothers. I didn't realize that the life I was living wasn't what everyone else experienced. I often felt that life wasn't real and that days drifted by without any meaning. Life had no purpose, so I had no purpose.

Home wasn't a safe place because of my stepdad. He would beat up my mum on a regular basis and then sometimes would start on my younger brother and me. He would drink heavily and then get angry with us. Sometimes he would beat us up simply because he was bored and wanted to do something. On one occasion, he beat up my mum because his dinner wasn't served in the right way; on other occasions, he just didn't need an excuse.

Because my stepdad was violent, my mum often became violent also and it was like she lashed out at us because of him.

It wasn't just his violence that made me hate him; he also started to abuse me sexually. This started to happen more often, when my mum was out. I tried to talk to my mum about what was happening but she didn't believe me and started to call me a slag for making such a thing up. My mum thought I was saying it because I was jealous of their relationship and that the whole thing wasn't true.

After years of this I felt as if I couldn't trust anyone. I felt worthless and powerless, but felt brave for taking this from him. I also felt that if I kept taking this from him it might save my younger brother from the same thing; somehow, I justified what was happening, in my own mind.

At the age of 10, I joined a gang which made me feel safe – they gave me a purpose and value. It made me feel powerful and important, as I was one of the ringleaders. We would often go out and take our hurt out on someone else; we would beat up random strangers and leave them in the park to sort themselves out. The gang was joined by older guys who started to ask me to do other things for them. I would go and sell drugs and other times they would tell me to go round to a guy's house and do whatever he asked me to do. This group became my new family and they made me feel wanted, even though I now know that they didn't want me, they just wanted me for what I could do for them. To cope with the pain of home and what I was doing with these guys, I started to take drugs to numb the pain, to stop me thinking about what was happening in my life; to make it all go away.

One summer a number of years ago, I met a group of young people who were running a small music festival in the park. They seemed to be a nice group – I noted very quickly that they were interested in me not because of what I could do for them, but because they thought I was OK; they didn't judge me or my life.

Over a period of time I got to know this group and spent time hanging out with them. They showed me love and acceptance that was different from the acceptance I had experienced in the gang. They wanted nothing from me, they just wanted to get to know me, find out who I was.

After a while they turned out to be Christians and were part of a local church, although this didn't seem to be on their agenda, they didn't want me to join their club. One of the girls started to chat to me about life at home and my stepdad and offered to take me to the police. Three times she went with me and each time I ran away, hoping the whole thing would simply go away. Someone else from the church offered to meet for food and hang out; we never talked God stuff but they showed interest in helping me get my life on track. They were interested in me and wanted friendship, this blew my mind. Over a period of time, they helped me get off the drugs, leave the gang and find another life.

This same group found me a new place to live away from the family and gang so I could start to live a better life. In the summer of 2006, I realized who Jesus was and what he had come to do. This group of Christians had shown me Jesus without even saying it, they had walked me through the mess and helped me in the same way Jesus would have. When I asked to be baptized they were so excited – they never expected me to want to make such a commitment to God, they just wanted to show me a new way of living. It wasn't that they didn't want me to become a Christian, but they wanted to show me God and his power to take a broken thing and reform it in a way that really applied to my life. I realized that Jesus' death meant I could be free from all the stuff I had been through.

Don't get me wrong, the old gang still find me now and again and now use me as a punch bag and my relationship with my mum is almost non-existent. But each day I see God working through this group around me. I have recently seen others experiencing this love as they have come to experience this Jesus community. I have seen others not judged but welcomed in; it's weird to see what happened to me happen to others, but this time I'm a part of it.

5.

The Resurrection Community

So, friends, every day do something
that won't compute. Love the Lord.
Love the world. Work for nothing.
Take all that you have and be poor.
Love someone who does not deserve it.
Denounce the government and embrace
the people. Hope to live in that free
republic for which it stands.
Give your approval to all you cannot
understand. Praise ignorance, for what man
has not encountered he has not destroyed.

Expect the end of the world. Laugh.
Laughter is immeasurable. Be joyful
Though you have considered all the facts . . .

. . . Practice resurrection.

A new *ekklesia*

The Roman Empire, led by the Caesar, was this evil dictating and oppressive force in the world. If you needed to get on in life you would need to live and breathe in the rhythm of the empire. You would have to be willing at any moment to say 'Caesar is Lord' and worship their gods in the empire's worshipping centres called *ekklesia*, or churches. This Roman world was powered by people who used others' shortcomings to make themselves look more powerful; they would claim authority over people and things to show their strength. It was about becoming a celebrity, or famous for doing 'that thing' or being in 'this place', and all of this was led by a man who claimed to be God. It was a world powered by the upward spiral of the important, grasping at others in the hope of being able to climb higher up the Imperial ladder.

Peter, a very ordinary guy, the kind you would see down the pub after a hard day at work, had been signed up into Jesus' little group that was starting to see the world in a very different way. Jesus had presented them with a new way of living; a world where the poor came first and the wealthy would be last. A world that contradicted the empire of this world, led by men. A world where it wasn't about being religious, but about relationships and people. And a world not about grasping at others to climb up the Imperial ladder. This was a world of non-grasping, neutral serving and giving of self for the benefit of others.

Three years before Jesus died he had started his ministry at a local synagogue in Galilee. At this synagogue Jesus stood up to read from the scroll of Isaiah and read a section as if it were his mission statement for his ministry. He read: "God's Spirit is on me; he's chosen me to preach the Message of good news to the poor, Sent me to announce pardon to prisoners and recovery of sight to the blind, To set the burdened and battered free, to announce, "This is God's year to act!"' (Luke 4:16, *The Message*)

Jesus' mission was to set the burdened and battered free, give new sight, new healing, and new life. And he announced that it was God's year to act. This was Jesus' mission; his mission was an active mission, a particip-atory mission and he set out to find a band of men who would join him in setting the battered free, giving new sight and being proactive.

Three years later, Jesus sits in front of this very normal bloke, a bloke who in recent weeks had become battered himself but had also seen this Jesus movement come to life in Jesus' death and resurrection. Jesus sits with Peter and invites him to not only lead his people, but set up Jesus' own *ekklesia*, church.

Jesus' *ekklesia* would not be like that of the empire. Caesar's system was an aggressive military organization, a passive political system and an apathetic liberator. Jesus wanted to set the battered and bruised free; he wanted a movement that would act on injustice, a movement that would participate in the resurrection of the world. He wanted a movement of people who were all dying to their own desires so that they could preach good news, announce pardon, recover sight and bring freedom to the battered. This new *ekklesia* was always intended to be not only an active movement bringing life to a spiritually dead world, but also bringing life to a physically dead world.

Jesus gave Peter the job of starting his *ekklesia* which was to be Jesus on earth. The very way Jesus would be able to reveal his resurrection to the empire and to the world was through the church. This church was a group of people who had experienced the resurrection and now were calling others into it.

Living upside down

Peter had firsthand experience of the power of the resurrection. Imagine Peter spending three years of his life seeing Jesus living out his upside down world, and deciding to live this out too. Peter had been sent out to serve with the other disciples he had seen the sick healed and those emotionally worn down put back together. Then hours before Jesus' death, Peter realizes the full significance of being a part of this Jesus movement. Jesus is being led to an illegal trial and Peter finds everyone turning on his leader. The questions going through Peter's mind may have been 'Will I be next?', 'Will I be taken like this?' and 'Will I be led to my death?' Peter wanted to commit to a movement that would help others, but was not yet ready to commit to a movement that would mean he also needed to die.

On three occasions, different people come to Peter, recognizing him as one of Jesus' rabble, and three times he tries to avoid going down the same road by distancing himself from Jesus. Peter lies, trying to avoid his death; he could not see how this could ever work out well for Jesus' new movement. How could someone weak beat someone as strong as the empire?

Each time Peter says he doesn't know who Jesus is. On the third occasion, he has been asked if he is one of Jesus' men and Peter's response is totally the opposite to wanting to follow Jesus. Peter's fear causes him to call down curses on himself and he begins to swear to them that he doesn't know Jesus.

Have you ever seen someone lying through their teeth trying to get away from being caught? Recently my church was running a Saturday night café-style gig. On tables there were silly children's games that anyone could play. However, there had been one guy who had kept taking bits of the games and putting them in his pocket. Seeing him stuff more plastic coins in his coat pocket I approached him and asked him to put them back on the table; the young guy was busted. He had been caught red-handed and there was no way of denying it had been him. I politely asked him for the coins back and he lied to my face saying he hadn't ever been by the games and it must have been someone else. He went as far to say that he didn't even know there were games on the tables and that people were always out to get him. Over a few minutes he lied over and over, telling me that I was the one lying in the hope of getting him in trouble. His face was desperate, he was eyeing up the door, working out his getaway plan like it was some bank job, looking for someone to step in and bail him out. He was scared and, in his fear of being caught with ten plastic coins in his hand, he made a run for the door.

Have you ever been in a situation where you were almost caught red-handed and busted for lying?

Peter denies Jesus three times, and on the third time he curses himself. Peter is practically saying, 'Let me die if I am lying. I don't know him.' Peter calls death on himself; he is scared and worried.

Peter experiences his rabbi dying the following day . . . all alone.

Peter has nowhere to go. The movement is over, Jesus has gone and he is left with no place to go. So he heads back to Galilee. He heads home, back to his old life, burdened by the knowledge that he left his friend in the last moments of his life, bruised by his own behaviour, bruised and looking silly for committing to a rebel who has been killed by the empire.

Peter returns home and goes back to fishing. But a few days later, after Jesus' resurrection, Peter finds himself having breakfast with him. Imagine how stupid he must have felt, knowing that his rabbi knew he had done a runner and denied ever knowing him, even calling death on himself.

Jesus then shows us what true resurrection power is by turning to Peter three times and asking him if he loves him. Three times he denies Jesus, so three times Jesus puts him back together. Jesus is in the business of resurrection, not wounding us even more. Jesus could have argued with Peter, got him to make amends for being such a bad friend, but he doesn't. Jesus practises resurrection on Peter and puts him back in shalom with him, and then invites him to start his *ekklesia* that will practise resurrection; the resurrection that Peter has now experienced firsthand.

The first mega church

Peter does as he is told. In Acts 2, we see him standing right in the middle of the religious empire addressing the gathered crowd and bringing 3,000 to faith. In Acts 2:42–45, we see what this new Jesus movement looks like: 'They devoted themselves to the apostles' teaching and to the fellowship, to the breaking of bread and to prayer. Everyone was filled with awe, and many wonders and miraculous signs were done by the apostles. All the believers were together and had everything in common. Selling their possessions and goods, they gave to anyone as he had need.'

The word for fellowship used by Luke in the description is the Greek word *koinonia* which means 'sharing in' or 'joining in'. They knew that they could not practise resurrection unless they were doing it together. We are also told that they had 'everything in common'. To live sharing everything with someone else is a deeply challenging concept. They gave up their own rights for the rights of others; to have everything in common is to be equal with someone but to purposefully make yourself less important. This was a group of people who were giving up everything so that they could be a part of this community. This community was the total opposite to Affluenza; it was about others, about becoming smaller so others would be more important and about the downward spiral of ascent.

Lately, I have found myself reading some of the old church fathers and came across this fantastic quote from a Greek Roman historian. Aristides wrote to the emperor in AD 137 about the behaviour of Christians. Artistides writes:

Oh emperor, it is the Christians that have sought and found the truth, for they acknowledge God. They do not keep for themselves the goods entrusted to them. They do not covet what belongs to others, but they show love to their neighbours. They do not do to another what they would not like done to themselves. They speak gently to those who oppress them, and in this way, they make their enemies their friends. It has become their passion to do good to their enemies. They live in the awareness of their own smallness. Everyone of them who has anything gives ungrudgingly to the one who has nothing. And if any of them sees a homeless stranger, they bring them into their own home, under their roof. If any one of them becomes poor while the Christians have nothing to spare, then they fast two or three days until everyone can eat. In this way, they supply for the poor exactly what they need. This, oh emperor, is the rule of life for the Christians. This is how they live.

Love it. Anyone want to come with me to this kind of community?

In your going

For many people, this very new Christian community just didn't compute. It was in total contradiction to the world the empire had set up – to an outsider it would have just looked ridiculous. Almost like a king riding into a city on the back of a donkey the size of a child's bike kind of ridiculous.

This would have been LOL (laugh out loud).

The empire's response was to ignore it as much as they could. They hoped it would simply implode and cease once people came back to their right minds. But what if it wasn't the empire that was in its right mind, but this new Jesus community? What if it was the world that had gone mad?

Just before Jesus ascended into heaven he met with his followers in Galilee and told them something. This event is generally called the Great Commission and it was when he told his small band of revolutionaries what he wanted them to do. In Matthew 28:18,19 Jesus turns to the disciples and says, 'All authority in heaven and earth has been given to me. Therefore go and make disciples of all nations'.

The phrase 'Therefore go' isn't the best translation of the Greek *poreuthentes auv*. A better way of saying it would be '*in your going* make disciples', yet even that isn't a great translation. A more accurate understanding of the phrase would be '*where you have been, where you are and where you are going*, make disciples'.

Where you were yesterday, where you are today and where you will be tomorrow. Your rhythm should be to bring people to life, to show them Jesus in his resurrection brilliance.

In other words, your whole rhythm of life should be to resurrect people, and practise resurrection.

The modern church has become about yearly mission weekends, nights when the church puts on events and invites people to non-Christian-friendly gatherings. Jesus never told his church to invade the world once a year, or to try to convince people they are 'normal' at barn dances. Jesus' church was never normal compared to the world; compared to the empire.

Jesus wants his church to practise his resurrection power, the power that changes people, things, animals and atoms, right here, right now, today.

As Wendell Berry, the poet, has already said:

. . . every day do something
that won't compute. Love the Lord.
Love the world. Work for nothing.
Take all that you have and be poor.
Love someone who does not deserve it.
Denounce the government and embrace
the people. . . .
. . . Practice resurrection.

Too battered to resurrect anyone

The church, Jesus' *ekklesia*, needs to relearn what it means to practise resurrection. That could sound too challenging since many of us can't resurrect anyone and often can barely get through our own day. This is why it is so important for us to remember that practising resurrection is not about us, it is about Jesus working in and through us. It's about Jesus giving us his Spirit to empower us and work through us. The Spirit is a new life birthed in us, an inner force propelling us along when previously the batteries had died. In John 3:3 we learn that this Spirit is a new vision, a new heart, a new passion for Jesus' kingdom.

Jean Vanier, founder of L'Arche, a community for people with developmental disabilities, writes in his book *Drawn into the Mystery of Jesus Through the Gospel of John* that this empowering and restoring Spirit is 'a new freedom that separates us from the ways and influences of the world so that we will no longer be enslaved in fear and greed, craving money and power' but empowered to restore lives.

It's this same Spirit that reminds us of Jesus' strength, Jesus' depth. The Spirit forms us so that the only natural and normal thing to do is serve others. Everything else becomes a waste of time – even when we don't have the energy, even when we struggle to get through the day. The Spirit in us makes all things possible.

Resurrection is the returning of a life that has been lost or taken; practising resurrection is, in fact, about bringing to life what has been lost because of *chatta't* by the resurrection power being at work.

Peter could not resurrect anyone because he was battered, bruised and broken. But three times Jesus put Peter back together and Jesus wouldn't have stopped there, he would have sat there all day putting Peter back together if he needed to. But the point is, Peter only went on to practise resurrection because of Jesus' power in him. The Holy Spirit given to Peter at Pentecost was the resurrection power at work in him and then flowing into the world.

The modern church has become so well known for practising crucifixion, witch-hunting leaders who have fallen, and hunting down those who have varying sexual orientation. We see this in the lives of Christians who have been hunted down for being seen as too liberal or fundamental, or those on the edges of the church who have been forced out because they're not seen as orthodox. We have hunted them, crucified them and stood back and patted ourselves on the back. Sometimes it is as though we have come full circle and the community Jesus was starting has become the one that now does the crucifying.

It sounds to me like we have become the corrupt religious empire.

We know how to crucify, but what does it mean for the church to practise life? The sight of life bursting into this world has yet to be seen on the cover of *The Big Issue* or a tabloid newspaper.

It is very difficult to clearly express what practising resurrection is; it is much easier to point to it. To see it happen and then say, 'That's it.'

The power of Easter

Practising resurrection is about practising the life of Jesus, the power of Easter, wherever you are; at the mall, at football with the kids, or in the queue at the petrol station. Practising resurrection is about being citizens of Jesus' empire. It is loving our enemies: both our global enemies, like terrorists and kidnappers, and our personal enemies, like the annoying neighbour whose dog barks all night, the difficult family member who is always speaking without thinking, or the person at work who talks badly about us to the other staff. Practising resurrection means loving all of these, and loving them means seeing them in their death and helping to bring resurrection life to them with Jesus. It's about seeing why that staff member is speaking badly about us and helping them work through it.

I recently heard about a family whose relationships had broken down to the extent that they were no longer speaking. After eight years they once again resumed contact, all because the youngest son had decided he needed to step in and be resurrection in the broken relationship. He started to go round each family member speaking well of the others; he used his own time, time that he would have used to be with friends, to speak highly of each and every member of the large family. Over a period of a year and a half he started to get younger family members speaking and this snowballed into the whole family speaking. This family now spends significant chunks of time together.

I have a friend who grew up in a very wealthy family and was a graduate of a business degree. In her mid-twenties, she decided to break out of that rhythm of life and to move out of her comfy church and become church on a tough estate. She moved with a group of friends and decided to meet and worship a couple times a month, but on the other weeks would try to serve the people they were now living with. Over time they became key members of the community and would help the other residents in whatever way they could. On one occasion, my friend stopped to help an older gentleman with his shopping bags, the guy invited her in for a cuppa so she accepted. After sitting with him for an hour, he turned to her and said that she was the first person to come into his home and spend time with him in the fifteen years that he had lived on the estate.

Just one coat

On one occasion, my friend went to see if they could help a mother and daughter equip their home with the basics that they needed. The mother and daughter were refugees who had fled a war zone and now lived in one of the flats on the estate. All the mother and daughter had was one coat which the small daughter was now sleeping on; the mother was on the floor.

Poverty is not just in the Third World, it's not only found in other countries, it is also found on our own streets and our own estates. Poverty is right here because people have been relocated for many reasons beyond their own control. My friend went to a Christian charity which rehomes furniture that has been donated, and they kitted the small family out with everything they needed.

On some occasions they repaint people's kitchens and living rooms, other times they get people beds or teach English to refugees, and other times they simply go carol singing.

Before my friend moved onto the estate, she heard God tell her to love people back to life. She dreamed of being Jesus' hands, feet and heart and decided to live it out, practise resurrection right there where she lived.

I know this woman who lives in a block of flats in London with her husband; their neighbours are a mixture of people from all walks of life. On one occasion, the woman started a conversation with a neighbour who told them how they were struggling; the father had been made redundant, the mother was unable to find work because of visa issues and this family had three young children to feed.

The couple dashed into their flat, put on their coats and invited the mother to come shopping with them to the local supermarket. The couple invited the woman to come and fill her trolley full with food and they would pay. The couple then said that they would take her shopping again in two weeks and then two weeks after that until the family had sorted their finances out.

The young mother could not believe or understand the love and cried, 'Thank you.'

Because Jesus came for them

A group of young people from my church have been working with our local council in spreading the word about anti-bullying. They have been going around to meetings and shopping centres saying that everyone is valuable, that life needs to be kept sacred and that people need us to speak out against anything which pushes and holds them down and takes away their freedom. They have produced mouse mats and groovy little information packs to try and communicate that 'Love Wins'. In one meeting, a council worker asked why these young people were so passionate about anti-bullying and one of the young people replied, 'Because Jesus spoke out for the battered and the bruised, and so will we.'

A few weeks later, I was sat having coffee with someone who had been in the room and heard this, and she began to ask about this Jesus. She wanted to know why the Jesus the young people spoke of had a practical day to day reality and why they felt their faith had everything to do with anti-bullying.

Later in the conversation she said, 'I didn't realize Jesus' message was still so alive, I thought the church had killed it.'

At the last anti-bullying event, held in the local shopping centre, my church had booked bands to come and provide music that would communicate a new message about bullying. As the music was playing, members of the church spoke to young people and asked them about their experience of bullying and gave out information about who they could speak to.

As two of the guys han-ded one lad some information, his mother asked where they were from. When they told her, the mother gave back the anti-bullying information saying to her son they were from a cult. The two young people came to me and told me everything that had happened and I couldn't help but laugh. This was brilliant, this was the best news I had heard all year; I was leading a cult. The word cult literally means to 'cultivate another culture' and this is what we want to do. We want to cultivate a new culture where everyone is valued, we do things that set people free, for free. This message is alien to the world, so yes, we look like a cult.

I am thinking about changing my work title from church leader to cult leader, it has a more Jesus movement feel to me, but I'm not sure people will understand where we are coming from.

Resurrection work

I have this friend who studied as a web designer and now owns and runs her own web design agency that tends to specialize in charity websites. This friend is very passionate about justice, the poor and the oppressed and has been desperate to help others speak out about the terrible behaviour of some large companies. After many hours of thought she came up with the idea of an attachment to a social networking site what would allow people to send pre-written emails to large clothing firms, chocolate manufacturers or even the Prime Minister. The attachment, called SuperBadger, was picked up by Tearfund and now gives the opportunity to badger people about ethical issues.

Whether it's badgering politicians about climate change or badgering supermarkets to stock more Fairtrade products, SuperBadger invites people to speak out about such things. Roughly every two weeks a new badger is uploaded, and sending the badgers gets you points so that you can become a SuperBadger. Super-Badger successfully got Thorntons to stock Fairtrade, and Cadburys soon followed suit.

I was away having a few days of quiet back in the beginning of the year, and at the monastery I was staying at there was a nun who offered foot massages for those on retreat. There was no way I couldn't take up the offer so I headed down to the little room which the Sister used for the session. As I arrived, the Sister was beaming and ready for me and a conversation kicked off. It turned out that this Sister had been living in the monastery for the last forty years and that she had decided to go to an evening class for massage, specializing in foot massage.

When she had finished the training, she decided to take her new skill down to the local food programme that worked with the homeless of South London. The Sister offered time to serve those needing food, and for those who wanted to stay longer she offered to clean, massage and treat their feet. Each day she would stay around for four to five hours treating the feet of people that hadn't showered in months. She shared how this foot-massaging ministry had been the most profound teaching in her life; she had learnt to wash the feet of those who no one else wanted to wash. As the session ended, she leant towards me and said, 'We need to learn to love without getting tired.'

Those words have stuck with me, and I have made her message a personal one. I, Cris Rogers, need to learn to love without getting tired, and I invite you to join me.

We aren't going anywhere

In the news recently, there was a story of an aid worker in Iran who had been killed for being a Christian. Her work in Iran was through a charity that aimed to feed and clothe those affected by the war, and find new homes for children left parentless.

The worker had been in Iran for many years and had earned the respect of many local Muslims as someone who really cared, but one group had decided she was simply there to convert people.

The news story on the front page of the papers read 'Death of a Good Samaritan'. The story went on that the woman had been shot and that local charities were recommending that other workers leave the area and find work in safer places. The response from the Christian Aid workers was completely the opposite; they said that they would commit to staying and helping those who were in deep need, even if it meant that they, too, would be killed.

The aid workers committed to stay in a place where they could die, but knew that their work, bringing resurrection life to those beaten, bruised and damaged, was worth the sacrifice.

I am aware of churches which are taking large chunks of their buildings and turning them into medical practices, food-serving programmes and financial help centres. I am aware of one church doing a deal with local builders to build them a centre to house people who have been kicked out of home; the centre now houses pregnant teens and those who are at risk of social exclusion.

Simple resurrection

Practising resurrection doesn't have to be that big, it can be a simple way of sharing resurrection life, and we can all be involved. We need to think of fresh and creative ways of bringing the power of the Easter story into this dead world, daily. Practising resurrection is about being a daily reminder that death in all its forms is not acceptable and that death does not have the final word: Jesus and his resurrection have the final word.

Practising resurrection isn't merely about trying to do random acts of kindness, it's about being empowered to love and live in the life-giving energy found in the resurrection.

It's about being the one who starts the conversation to reconciliation, allowing our own ego and pride to die so that we can see life come in someone else. It's about seeing the opportunity to put on our coats and go shopping with a near-stranger. It's about staying in the place which could ultimately cause us death to bring life to others. It's about the willingness to use our time creatively to speak out against the poor and the oppressed. It's about seeing where there is death, and loving people back to life. It's about picking up the old guy's shopping and sitting for hours as he tells us we're the only person to come and visit him in fifteen years. It's about picking up the paintbrush and creating a space that makes people feel there is a life worth living. It's about doing this because we are less important, it's because Jesus is resurrecting us, it's about us being Jesus' hands, love and heart.

Eucharizomi

You can walk into any church in the world and there is one event that binds them all together. The sung worship would be different, so would the style of communication and even the quality of the coffee and biscuits. But there is one event that will happen all around the world as chur-ches come together. This event goes by many names. Some call it communion, some the Lord's Supper, some even the family meal, and others call it the Eucharist. Not only the name varies, so does both the frequency and the style in which it is done. But at the end of the day, it is the same meal. This meal dates back to Moses' time when the people of God were trapped in Egypt. God had promised to set them free and one night warned them to take a lamb and paint its blood on the doorposts of their houses. Not the kind of decorating you would find on some TV house renovating programme with an overdramatic presenter.

The story goes that death visited Egypt and where it found the blood of a spotless lamb it passed over; where it didn't, the firstborn male of the family died.

It was the blood of a spotless sacrifice that indicated that death was not welcome here.

Later in the story, the people of God, now free from the tyranny of Egypt, were wandering in the desert. This nomadic group were starving and in desperate need of food, so God promised to give them bread and it came every morning in the form of manna. In Exodus 16 the manna was found on the ground and when the people came out of their tents and saw it they didn't quite know what to say. The Hebrew for manna literally translates as 'Eh?' The bread from heaven became known as 'Eh?' They had no idea what this was, the bread was nothing like anything they had eaten before, and they called it 'Eh?', or you could say, 'What is it?'

In Egypt, the blood of the lamb said death was not welcome here, and in the desert the bread communicated God's provision.

Years later Jesus, like all the other good Jews, sat remembering this story in a meal and the meal was called the Passover. In the meal, they remembered God's blessing, his provision. They remembered the 'What is it?' and they remembered how God always came through for them.

As Jesus goes through the meal with his friends, singing and speaking, he redefines two of the main elements of the meal. Firstly, the wine they drank to remember the doorposts and the lamb's blood. Jesus now uses these to communicate his blood as the blood that says death is no longer welcome here. He then takes the bread that reminded them of God's provision in hard times and he likens this to his body providing for them.

Blood poured out and the body was broken not just for the people of Egypt but the people of the world. This meal became

known as the Eucharist. Eucharist comes from the Greek word
eucharizomai:

eu – good
charizomai – give or gift

The Eucharist is God's good gift, Jesus is the good gift.

Poured and broken

On the cross, Jesus' body is broken and his blood poured out
for the world. Jesus is our Eucharist; good gift. Remember back
in Colossians 1:20 it said that Jesus' death came to bring
shalom, peace, and that this peace affected not only sin but
people, things, animals and even the atom.

Jesus makes *shalom* with the whole of the world and the
whole of the universe through his Eucharist, through his good
gift.

Jesus allowed his body to be broken and his blood to be
poured out because he was faithful to his mission. He was
faithful to his mission to bring *shalom* to his people, Jew and
Gentile, to those near and those far off.

Now Jesus invites us to pick up our cross and follow him. He
invites us to pick up our cross and be 'body broken and blood
poured out' for the world. He calls us to be Eucharist. Good
gifts for the world.

We need to see that we are now invited to be 'Eucharists'
with Jesus. We need to allow things to die in us so that he will
be raised in us. We need to be broken and poured out.

If we want to see the poor fed, then one of Jesus' Eucharists
needs to be willing to give. If we want to see people set free,
then one of Jesus' Eucharists needs to be willing to fight for
their freedom. If we want to see poverty crushed and the
homeless housed, then one of Jesus' Eucharists needs to be

willing to step in and be their voice. For someone on the underside to receive something, then someone has to pay something.

It's through our giving that we give life to others. It is through Jesus' broken body that the world can be healed.

And the body of Christ is us and we need to be broken.

The church is a group of people all living the Eucharist, being broken and poured out for the healing of the world. People all freely allowing their bodies to be broken and their blood poured out to see the healing of the nations.

In the early twentieth century there was an Archbishop of Canterbury called William Temple. Temple, in a moment of brilliance, said that 'The Church is the only society on earth that exists for the benefit of non-members'.

The church never existed for its own sake or the sake of the members. Jesus started his own *ekklesia* in opposition to the Roman *ekklesia*. This *ekklesia* existed to be broken and poured out, not for its own entertainment but for the healing of the world. The church exists not for our benefit, but theirs.

Thinking deeper

- Are our social circles anything like that of Jesus? Who is it that we spend most of our time with?
- How can we live as we do when they live as they do? What changes do we need to make to be resurrection to those who live in poverty right on our doorstep?
- What does it look like for you to be Eucharist right where you are?
- Have you ever practised resurrection like in the stories found in this chapter? What led up to you being willing to serve in this way?
- What is the deepest need in your community? What would need to happen to totally eradicate it?
- Could you be a part of the resurrection movement that did in fact eradicate the problem?
- Have you ever avoided speaking to someone because you know it's going to use up time that you need to do your own thing? How can you become someone who gives their time more freely to those in need?

Example of resurrection: Five

A real-life story about a man named Dick and another man named Ramtin Soodmand:

On 12 October 2008 I was at home drinking a relaxing cup of coffee, reading the Sunday paper, glancing from story to story, when my attention fell upon an article about a man called Ramtin Soodmand who was in prison in Meshed, north-eastern Iran. Ramtin was a Christian who had been brought up a practising Muslim. Now in prison, he hadn't been charged with any crime but the worry was that the Iranian parliament had just voted overwhelmingly – 196 to 7 – to press ahead with a bill to enshrine into law the Shariah death penalty for any male who had converted from Islam to any other religion.

The article had a photo of Ramtin and his wife and beautiful little daughter all sitting on a sofa in happier days. It also showed his worried sister who now lives in London and his father, an ordained minister who was hanged in 1990 for refusing to deny his faith.

Sitting at home in the Midlands I knew I had to do something. So I sat down to write to the Foreign Secretary, my local MP and my MEPs. I wrote a letter to the Iranian Ambassador and decided to jump on a coach down to London that following Thursday (16 October).

So, on a nice sunny Thursday morning, I made it to the Iranian Embassy on the south side of Hyde Park almost next door to the Royal Albert Hall. This was the place that the SAS had stormed a few years back.

I pressed the button and waited for a reply. The door clicked and I entered into this amazing embassy lobby with its reception desk. It turned out that the Ambassador was out on business and that the man I needed to see was the Legal Affairs Attaché; he wasn't available to see me either, but they did let me leave my letter with them. I wasn't in any hurry to push off only a few seconds into my visit, but I hadn't seriously imagined they'd see me there and then.

Deciding that it would be good to meet the Attaché, I asked for his number which they surprisingly gave me, so I went to do some shopping and decided to keep ringing the number on my mobile. I eventually got through and he agreed to see me the following Tuesday – 21 October – back at the embassy. As the day was getting late, I returned home to wait for my appointment the following week.

I woke early on the Tuesday and jumped on the first coach to London. The embassy door swung open and the reception-ist was there with a handwritten note. The Attaché was very sorry but he had been called away to an 'important meeting'. He couldn't see me that day and could we make another appointment for another day. This was rubbish. I felt that I had been fobbed off, strung along, and I wasn't going to let them waste my time, so I decided to dig my heels in.

'I'd like to see His Excellency the Ambassador, please.'

This was no good so I decided to ask if they could get the Attaché on his mobile which they declined to do, telling me that they didn't actually have his mobile number. I told them that I thought this was ridiculous as they had given me his mobile num-ber the week before! They then told me that he would be out all day and that they would contact me with a new date. I said that wasn't good enough. Then they said that he would be returning later in the day. Jumping on this information, I said this was fine and that I would wait until he returned. To the receptionist's hor-ror I sat down in the waiting room. The small room had a loo and I had a bottle of water and a packet of mixed peel like you put in a Christmas cake, and with this I settled down for a long wait.

Soon they got word that he wouldn't be back until late in the day, maybe 6 or 7 in the evening. My response was that I was glad it wasn't going to be an overnight camp-out job in this little room. The packet of peel wouldn't last that long.

I sat in the room waiting and praying that God would work in the situation, I rang around friends asking them all to pray, and I even rang the church office, letting them know what was happening if I never reappeared – which now feels a little melodramatic.

I sat reading a book I had brought, the sun started to set and the steady stream of people coming for visas slowed down. Eventually the staff brought me a coffee as they realized I was there to stay.

Eventually at 6 p.m. the door swung open and the Attaché walked into the lobby. He was charming and very apologetic for the situation.

I looked him in the eye and said, 'I don't want this man hanged and I want your parliament to drop its plans about hanging Christians, please. You need these people, they are good citizens and they should be allowed to play a full part in the life of your country and be accorded their full human rights . . .' Etc. etc. etc. The rant went on and ended with me thanking him for hearing what I had to say.

We parted on good terms and I rang home to let them know I was leaving alive and safe! I had missed my seat on the coach but they kindly let me on a later one after I explained what I had been to London for. I rode home hoping that my time hadn't been wasted and that some good had come of it, even though I felt like a painful lone voice.

I decided to try to get others praying and writing letters, but people were busy and said that they would maybe help next time.

On 9 November the whole thing was still on my mind and at our church prayer night I heard someone pray for Ramtin. I realized that I could not let this drop; I still needed to do something. I started to ring around people I knew asking them to pray and to dig around for fresh information. In the end, I rang a charity that reports on such global tragedies as these. The woman on the phone was really friendly and reported that she thought he had been released sometime in October. I did more digging and it was correct, Ramtin had been freed.

Ramtin Soodmand had been released on 22 October 2008. I checked my wall diary by my desk as I tried to orientate myself to the timeline of events. The article had been printed on 12 October; my visit was on 16 October, so the long day at the Embassy had been the . . . yes, the 21st, ending at 6.30 p.m., or 10 p.m. Iran-time. Ramtin had been released the very next day, the 22nd. I was so pleased! My time off work hadn't been wasted, God had used my sacrifice of time, and Ramtin was free less than twenty-four hours after my camp-out in the embassy.

I'm now thinking about how to do the same to get the whole Islamic Penal Code Bill dropped quietly, but that's going to have to be a whole other trip to London . . .

6.

People of the Resurrection

In our world:

Hate is dominant.
Oppression is currency.
Violence is glorified.
Greed is praised.

But let it know of something different.
Something radical, something fresh.

That we will:

Clothe the naked.
Feed the hungry.
Uphold the meek.
Light the darkness.
Bring the dead to life.

Be the flame that lights the way;
The life that saves the dead.

Resurrection is in our hands.

'In Our Hands' by Jared Lovell (2009)

The long pause

I was standing in the class responding to question after question about Christianity. I was like a prize batsman on the cricket pitch. I was slogging them right over the heads of the fielders getting run after run. If 'heaven points' counted, I was out there collecting a lifetime's. I was teaching a GCSE class on Christianity and had been sharing how Jesus was an amazing revolutionary rabbi and not a hippie wearing a beauty pageant sash. It had gone really well as I talked through Middle Eastern understandings of some of Jesus' political teachings.

The lesson was almost over and the quiet girl raised her hand for the first time. Rule Ten of teaching: It's never good to end with a quiet girl's question; it's guaranteed to be a curve ball. In the lesson I had talked about Jesus' resurrection and how he had also raised others from the dead. I had then concluded how Jesus invited his church to now be his hands and feet and wanted us to continue his work.

The girl looked like she had been brewing this question for some time and, as there were no others hands left, I nodded to hear her question.

'Have you ever resurrected anyone?'

I paused. If I said no then would I be fuelling her argument that Christians today didn't do the kind of things Jesus did? Was it better to duck the question, or was it best to try to be honest? I paused for too long and she asked the question again; it was awkward.

The prize fighter

Naaman was a commander in the army of King Aram and was the kind of warrior all kings needed. Naaman was an *ish gadol* or mighty warrior, mighty fighter, prize soldier, and had given his king victory after victory.

An *ish gadol*, like Naaman, was the centrepiece of any army and would have eaten with the king on occasions if not more often. The Hebrew word *gadol* refers to the greatest man of the generation or the family; Naaman was the greatest military leader the king had in his kingdom. In the world of 2 Kings, Naaman was a celebrity, a well-loved, well cared-for, well-respected military leader. He would probably even have been at the king's side when other dignitaries came to visit, as a warning sign that this was how tough the army was.

The problem was that Naaman was not only a mighty warrior, the greatest of his generation, but he was also a *metzora*, a leper. It was impossible to be an *ish gadol* and be a *metzora*, no great military leader could also have leprosy. Leprosy said that you were a social outcast, sent outside of the village beyond the walls to hide from the view of all the people. Naaman was a disgraced mighty leader, someone who had fallen from grace, someone deeply loved but not able to be loved at the same time.

Around the time of the story, warriors had come back from the battlefield with treasures, both gold and silver and slaves, to be shared around. Naaman's wife had been given a young slave girl to help her around the home. The young girl enjoyed being a part of this family and wanted to help Naaman in getting medical treatment. She had originally been from Samaria and remembered a wacky prophet who had a reputation for speaking and doing the work of God. The young girl spoke of the prophet and soon Naaman was standing in front of his king asking for blessing to go and find the prophet. It was granted, along with a letter explaining to the king of Israel that Naaman needed healing, and was not an advance party or a scout for a future invasion.

Naaman's meeting with the king of Israel did not go smoothly; the king panicked and freaked out that this mighty warrior had come to him for healing. It was widely believed by Naaman and others in the Middle East that a king was the earthly representative of their god, so if the king could not heal Naaman as the representative of God, then who could? The king, knowing that he couldn't do anything for Naaman, stood up and, in a passionate comic moment, ripped his clothes from top to bottom.

It is interesting to note that they also ripped clothes when somebody was dead or had just died. The king was implying that they were dead because he couldn't grant the request.

The problem was that the king had forgotten who he was, he had forgotten who he represented, and blurted out, 'Am I God?' The correct answer was no, but he was the primary representative to the world of his God.

The king, having forgotten who he represented, was simply a man whose religion had become a badge on his sleeve, like this was his football team: Team YHVH United.

The king was in a panic; could this have been a trick? Could this man be trying it on with the king to see what he would do? Was this mighty warrior coming to kill him? The king was just another partially religious man whose faith didn't affect how he behaved or lived; he wasn't a man who spoke out or acted for God. His faith had crumbled down to a system of religious acts that didn't affect how he saw the world or who he was.

Elisha was a slightly odd character, a little like the weird uncle who never misses the family gathering . . . strange dress sense, bad timing when talking about bad news, and the ability to be totally interpersonally inept. Elisha's behaviour at times had been a little odd, but nevertheless he was a prophet who did hear clearly from God.

When Elisha heard what had happened he sent the king a message to send Naaman down to his little wooden hut. So Naaman went to Elisha. Making his way from the religious centre, he travelled down to this little hut in the middle of nowhere. Naaman had been expecting to find healing in God's religious representative, the king, and had travelled accordingly with his horse and chariots – or, in our modern understanding, tanks and Jeeps. Naaman arrived with his army and his military vehicles right on the doorstep of Elisha's little hut. Some might say Naaman's arrival was a little OTT.

Elisha peered through his window and, seeing the large military presence outside his house, he sent out a messenger to Naaman. Elisha recognized that he couldn't do anything in his own name or own power, but that it was God's power that would heal Naaman. Because of this, Elisha didn't need to even speak to Naaman, but Naaman needed to do what God wanted.

The messenger approached Naaman and his tank and Jeeps and told him to go wash seven times in the River Jordan. Imagine someone coming to you and telling you that the solution to your illness is to wash: 'So sorry, Naaman, you need to wash.'

It wasn't surprising that Naaman wasn't impressed; not only would this have been seen as offensive, but the River Jordan wasn't the nicest of rivers compared to those back in Naaman's home of Aram. Naaman wasn't happy and stormed off to his tank in a rage. Naaman didn't want to go wash, he didn't want to do something so normal, he wanted a holy man to do something great for him. Aram had a reputation for being a highly dramatized culture and shamans or holy men used grand theatrics in their work, with most events being held in the context of a big ceremony. Naaman wanted high dramatics, creative theatrics and a big ceremony; he didn't want to wash in such an ordinary, grotty river.

After Naaman's men convinced him to do the simple act, he made his way to the river and washed seven times. As Naaman came up out of the water for the seventh time, his skin was restored and was as soft as a young boy's. (It's all there in 2 Kgs. 5:14.)

Naaman received new life, new skin. It wasn't given because he was an *ish gadol* or because he had tanks and Jeeps. This new life wasn't found in drama or in theatrics. Neither was it found in grand ceremonies; new life was found in the simple day to day washing in the River Jordan.

Naaman had been looking to the big grand religious ceremony to heal him, but found it in a God who healed in a river through washing, and Elisha was simply the man who knew God's life and pointed to it.

The impact and depth of the story doesn't end there. Naaman returned to Elisha. Naaman's king was understood to represent the local deity in Aram which was the god Rimmon — who was also known by the name Baal. Rimmon was known for his fertility and his healing of skin diseases. Naaman had travelled from his land, where the local deity's supposed ability was healing, to Israel where another God had healed him. Naaman realized at this point that there was no other God in the whole world other than the God Elisha served. Naaman had been a worshipper of another god, he wasn't a part of the family of followers of YHVH, but this hadn't stopped Elisha pointing to new life in the God of Israel . . . and now Naaman wanted to worship him also.

Elisha understood the rhythm of his God, Elisha understood that his God was about the normal day to day miracles. Many of the miracles we see with the Gospels are done within the normal day to day work of Jesus. His healings were never in the context of a worship ceremony but were in the reality of the world.

The service stop and the Jewish pigs

There was one occasion Jesus had been travelling for hours and had stopped by a well, a small 'service stop', for a break. While he was sitting at the well, a woman of little importance, no significance and a bad reputation came to get water. The well was in Samaria and this woman was a Samaritan. The Jews often referred to the Samaritans as pigs, they were considered people who were half-breeds, and there was a deep rracial hatred for them. As the woman came to the well to get some water, she would have noticed this Jewish man. This man who, in her eyes, would see her as dirty, unclean, untrustworthy and of no significance, was sitting at her well and started to ask her for a drink of water.

The woman came to the well day after day to collect water for those who lived in her home, this was a normal day for her, and nothing religious was involved with this work. The problem was that she was the village outcast and so had to go collect water when there was no one else at the well – no one who could comment on who she really was.

Here was a woman who kept herself to herself, and probably not just on the outside but on the inside too. She hid the real pain of her life, ashamed, used and abused by so many men. Who was there she could trust? Who was there she could look at and see humanity at its best? The men she had been with didn't want her, they already had wives and families back home. They wanted her for what she could perform for them.

This was a woman who was locked in her own prison cell and could not see any hope of freedom. This was a woman with hopes, loves and fears, but had been and seen too much with too many men to believe there was something better.

A good Jewish man would have known she was going to the well alone and at the wrong time of the day. A good Jewish man would have also known that he should not speak to a Samaritan woman because she was unclean. But Jesus cut right through this and asked for a cup of water. It didn't take much to enter into this woman's story; there was no awkward 'Can I tell you about God?' kind of questions.

'May I have some water?' allowed Jesus to enter into her day to day routine.

Jesus spoke with her for a while and soon she was running back to her village, telling them about Christ. What did Jesus do with her? Was it simply small talk? The reality was that Jesus knew that this woman was broken and damaged, she had slept with many men and the one she was with now wasn't her husband either. She was an outcast but he spoke to her in a way that made her comfortable, welcomed and an equal with him. There was no hierarchy.

Jesus doesn't play the game

There are two significant things happening in this story. Firstly, it was unknown for a Jewish man to speak to a woman in public. Husbands wouldn't have spoken to their wives in public and certainly wouldn't have spoken to women at wells. Secondly, Jesus talks theology with her, he allows her in on a theological conversation, which no dignified rabbi would have done. Jesus doesn't play the 'I'm a rabbi!' card.

The key to seeing what Jesus was doing with the woman is to understand who Jesus thought he was talking to. She wasn't a sinner, or a woman or even a Samaritan – she was a person.

Jesus gives this woman new life by making her human again, someone a person could be interested in not because you were talking about her sin, or for what she could do for you, but because she was human.

Jesus practises his resurrection life on her. She was dead with sin, dead to her community and probably dead emotionally from all the failed relationships. But Jesus takes her broken, dead life and makes her human again, makes her a person again, and shows her love again.

The resurrection life in her brought her to life and she runs back to the town; she runs back to the town made up of people she knows talk badly of her, she returns to the place she associates with death and she now brings life to it. In John 4:39

we read that many come to faith not because of what she says but because they can see a difference in her.

When people who are dead experience resurrection life it changes everything about them: They are now fully alive, fully real, fully human.

Sammy

Practising resurrection for Naaman was an event that was so normal: washing in the river like you would do every day. For the woman at the well, resurrection happened during one of her normal daily routines. Resurrection life isn't about the religious ceremonies, it's about Jesus' presence in the normality of the day.

Some time ago, I was visiting Bethlehem and was introduced to an older guy called Sammy. Sammy was a warm gentleman who was a part of the leadership of a small charity within the walls of Bethlehem called the House of Hope. Much of Bethlehem is now inhabited by Muslim families who often can't get the medical help they need for their children because of the 18-foot walls built around the town. The city is governed by the Palestinian National Authority which restricts people from entering and leaving the city walls. If a local resident wants to leave they have to queue, sometimes for hours and may not be allowed back in.

Sammy is a part of the House of Hope on the main street of Bethlehem that seeks to bring the good news of Jesus through spiritual and practical ministry to the blind, and physically and mentally handicapped of all ages in the city. Very few Christians now live in the city because living there has simply become too tough economically and emotionally. In the evening it is unsafe to walk the streets because Palestinian patrols roam around to find those who are maybe up to no good. The problem is that because people can't leave the city to get to work, they have to find work within the city walls and there just isn't enough for them all. The only money moving within the city is that which visitors bring with them when coming to visit the location of Jesus' birth.

There are many homeless children and sick children in the city that need help but have nowhere to turn. The House of Hope was set up to be the hands, feet and heart of Jesus right there in his own birthplace. It never planned to be a large, dramatic charity but wanted to work in the lives of people, which it does very well.

On one occasion, Sammy had had a call from a Muslim family whose child was very sick; the family didn't know who to turn to but had heard about Sammy. They knew he was a Christian and they knew that when he prayed his God answered his prayers. Sammy arrived at the home of the family to find a very sick child and he knew he needed to get him some medicine as soon as possible. Finding nothing, he knew he had to get out of the city walls and track down what he needed. Sammy waited until he heard the alarm to say the gates were open and that people could leave the city and then he was off as fast as he could to try and get back before they shut the gates two hours later.

Sammy drove as fast as possible to Jerusalem, sourced what he needed and got back to Bethlehem moments before the gates shut. He made his way back to the fam-ily and gave them what the boy needed; he also gave them some fresh food.

The father of the little boy asked Sammy to give him the medicine in the belief that maybe Sammy's God would be with his son if he gave the spoon of penicillin. Sammy prayed with the family and made his way back to the House of Hope. Several days later, the phone rang and the little boy was on the other end; the boy was back on his feet and feeling much better and had now started to eat again.

Sammy is working today in the streets of Bethlehem trying to be resurrection life to those who desperately need it.

Sammy also told me about what it was like to represent Jesus in the city at night. Sammy regularly goes out in his car to try to find children living on the streets, to take them back to the House of Hope, to feed them, clothe them and give them a place to sleep. There are children as young as 3 and 4 living on the streets of Bethlehem who have little hope of help.

On one occasion, Sammy left the house to drive around the city to find these children but was pulled over by one of the Palestinian street patrols. They tortured him in the street to find out what he was doing. Sammy was doing nothing illegal but they feared he might be a part of a group who were trying to rise up against the government. Sammy was electrocuted on his head by the patrol to try to get information from him; after finding nothing they sent him on his way.

Sammy to this day has the scars of these types of illegal interrogations on the streets but this never stops him going back out to help those who need the hope of Jesus.

Sammy is willing to serve in the everyday of his city, being the resurrection to children and families who know little of the true Christmas message originating from their city.

I name you daughter

The book of Lamentations is a collection of five poems, set after the destruction of King Solomon's Temple. The people were in exile, away from home for the second time, and they had to come to the realization that it was their behaviour that had caused them to be attacked and taken over.

Lamentations is a typical set of Jewish poems, with a narrator and several characters talking through their situation. In Lamentations 1:9 we come across a female who represents Jerusalem; God's beautiful city. In the verse it reads 'Her filthiness clung to her skirts; she did not consider her future.' Here we have a woman who has been through a lot, her past is clinging to her and because of it she cannot see any possible future. She is destined to be single and lonely for the rest of her days.

To understand quite the depth of her grief we need to understand what the writer is saying when he writes that she has filthiness clinging to her skirt. This phrase is a Jewish sexual euphemism and is telling the reader that this woman hasn't had relations with one man but many. It's the dirt of the ground where she has lain with other men that is now clinging to her. She has been sexually promiscuous and her past is catching up with her, her history is sticking to her very outer clothes and she has no way of avoiding it.

Don't we all come across women and men whose past is still sticking to them? It's like the road that they have been on is affecting the future that they can have. I've come across people who have been somewhere messy in their teens and then allowed this weight of dirt to stick to them right into their later years.

People like this have all kinds of names given to them: dirty, sluts, tarts, man-whores and prostitutes. These names begin to define not only how they see themselves but also how the world sees them, and eventually can result in them being unable to see a worthwhile future.

Often our language communicates how we see people or how they see themselves and this was exile, cast out, banished language.

In Lamentations 2:13 we now get to hear God speak into the situation, speaking over his outcast city: 'What can I say for you? With what can I compare you, O Daughter of Jerusalem? To what can I liken you, that I may comfort you, O Virgin Daughter of Zion?'

In Lamentations 1 she is an outcast, a woman with her history clinging to her filthy skirt, but now God steps forward and speaks over her and in one moment redefines his prostitute city.

God leans forward and calls her 'O Virgin Daughter'. God speaks new words over her, new words to redefine her and give her a new hope and future. No longer is she filthy but a virgin daughter.

Practising resurrection is when we choose to speak new, fresh life into someone. Giving them new defining words. It's when we take the sexually deviant, lean over the table and tell them that they are a pure child: 'You think you have screwed it up, you think you're a failure, you think you're abused, you think you are worthless, but I tell you that you're a spotless child of Zion.'

To acknowledge someone's pain, to hear them speak their failings and faults, to hear them speak about who and what has left them beaten and bruised is the first steps to their healing. To hear what they have been through, what life has been like for them, their story, the dirt of their skirt is the first step to their being redefined and rebuilt.

Practising resurrection is when we take someone who is far off, cast out, lost, battered and bruised, listen to their story and then give them a new name; new life is when we bring resurrection to them. Something new is birthed in them . . .

Hope.

We see this played out by Jesus time and again. People who are naturally out of the Abraham covenant because of skin diseases, and Levitical violations are pulled back in because of Jesus' action of love. He resurrects them.

In Matthew 9:20, a woman who has been bleeding for twelve years comes up behind Jesus and reaches out for healing. Leviticus 15:25 made it clear that any blood coming from a woman was unclean – she was dirty, filthy, cast out, and Jesus turns around and calls her 'daughter'.

Daughter was an invitation, pulling her back in. No longer out but hemmed in.

Over and over we see this rhythm: Jesus invites people back in because of what he says or because of how he acts.

The leper is touched.

The Samaritan woman is spoken to.

He has lunch with the tax collector.

And he saves the wedding from bringing shame on the family.

Jesus resurrects people by giving them a new name, a new identity, by simply loving them. When we choose to use inclusive language, when we give the outcast a hug, when we choose to rename the prostitute to daughter, we give new, resurrected life.

A number of years ago my wife, who is also a priest, was invited to take part in a TV programme on lap dancers in the Midlands. Not because she was one or had ever been to a club, but they wanted to have the church's voice in a programme looking at the life of a pole dancer.

Time after time in the interview my wife was asked how the church saw the women who worked in the clubs of the Midlands. Each time she gave an answer on how the church values relationships and focused upon positive messages of marriage and commitment. She also focused on the men that went and how they treated the women and their own girlfriends, who deserved more.

She talked about how each and every woman is a child of God and that he loved every one of them. He probably doesn't like how they earn money, but they were still daughters of the Creator.

They interviewed Beki for an hour on the topic but only one 30-second clip was used because what she said wasn't what they wanted. They wanted to get someone criticizing the women, beating them up further and telling them that they had to 'turn or burn'. This they didn't get from Beki, but they did get from another church leader who sadly tore strips off the women.

Beki tried to speak new words over the women – daughter, loved and beautiful – but someone else got the last word: sinner, outcast and filthy.

The church had an opportunity that day to have a new voice speak out, a voice like that of its founder, Jesus. Instead the harsh, pharisaic voice cried out:

SINNER

Practising resurrection is about bringing new dimensions of God's love over someone. Setting them free from the condemnation of their filthy skirt and redefining them as virgin daughters.

I sat having coffee with an old friend and they were taking about the work that they are doing at the moment. Their job is to find money for social transformation in the poorest areas in the UK. As the conversation went on, he paused and then revealed something I had never known about him. He sipped his coffee and said, 'Who'd have thought I would have ended up doing this?' He had trained in law so that he could pacify his family and make sure he was set up for life making money. Money was the reason to work; in biblical terms, he wanted to be a tax collector (someone who worked for the Romans and taxed more money so that they could become rich on the back of the empire). But since meeting with Jesus, he has had a new word spoken over him: generosity. Now he has been redefined by his new name, generous, and he seeks to help those who can't help themselves. He does this by putting in his own money.

Being the centre

It is in resurrection stories like Sammy's and my ex-tax collector friend's that we see what it means for salvation to come to those in the most need. If the cross is about everything changing, then it has to change people's lives, redeeming the broken parts so that they can then see how it changes the very brokenness of their own souls. Practising resurrection means the rebuilding of their whole lives so that they can see how their very soul needs rebuilding.

Sammy is *slowly* seeing people he has served come to faith as they see Jesus alive and well, working in him. The story of Jesus is the story of hope and the story of one man's death as an individual and his rising again as a community.

My church in West London is part of a team of three churches seeking to be the resurrection community that Jesus has called us to be. As a part of the team, we have a medical practice within the building of one of the traditional churches. This medical practice seeks to minister to people's health concerns in a practical way, as well as to their spirit.

Two thousand years ago, the small religious communities were centred on a synagogue. If you had a problem with health you would visit the synagogue; if you had financial problems – synagogue; schooling – synagogue; politics – synagogue; parties – synagogue; homeless – synagogue.

Everything centred on this synagogue building, with the idea of the religious community being there to speak God into whatever you needed. Everything was seen as spiritual; there was no concept of secular issues and religious issues because God was interested in your whole life. In the last 2,000 years, Christians and churches have succeeded in slowly separating the world in two: Religious stuff – you go to church; secular stuff – you go to the world, hospital, shops, Internet and government.

Two worlds

The Jewish idea of the world was that everything was integrated; there was no secular world or spiritual world, but they were both intertwined. Plato, the Greek philosopher, gave us the idea that there are two worlds. Firstly, one that is sacred or spiritual, which is good; one where the gods are, and therefore one we should all seek after. Secondly, the secular world, which is made up of the physical world. There is no god; everything is evil, dirty and sexually devious. Plato's Greek world-view makes the whole of life about learning to escape from the material world and head towards the spiritual, enlightened world.

Our Western world-view is formed by this Greek philosophy and this is why so often the Bible seems to make odd claims, or seems to sit opposed to the way we live. It is speaking of a world which sees itself as both sacred and secular at the same time, but we aren't able to hold these two things in tension.

We see religion as something that helps us to flee from the evil of this world into some kind of sacred holiness. This idea of how the world works means we end up with odd ideas such as this place over here is a church, therefore it is somehow more sacred than this park over here. God must be more present, somehow, in this holy place and less present in this secular place. This is why we find it so easy to turn on our Sunday-life and then turn it off again during our Monday-to-Saturday life. This is one reason why people find it easy to go out drinking and having sex with whoever on the Friday, or live with addictive behaviours, and then on the Sunday turn up to church. We also see this in Christian music compared to the secular music world; people talk about only buying Christian music, which must imply that God therefore can only work through Christian musicians.

Are you now reading a *Christian* book or are you reading a book?

We have to become conscious that everything is in the realm of God, and that nothing is outside his authority.

'In' the world

I was having a meeting with a youth worker friend who said that his young people needed to stop getting trapped in 'the world'.

The danger with this line of theology is that it can lead us down a path where we end up with a disembodied Christianity that is unable to engage with the whole of people's lives. We need a church that isn't hiding from the world but is nurturing and generating a people that know no distinction between the spiritual and the rest of life. The whole of life is God's arena; it is God's playground. Every aspect of life should be invaded by God.

We have a problem that for the last 150 years the church has struggled to engage with the deepest issues of this world because people have struggled to think deeply about their faith. The church has allowed a growing divide between itself and what happens on the streets, what happens in the council, what happens in health care and schooling.

This idea of being in the world but not of it has developed a church which has tried to hide away, striving to become more and more holy, separate from the outside world, a church which isn't dirty, worldly or secular. This line of thought has subtly created a Sunday-only Christianity. Matthew 5:14 tells us that we are the light in the world, but we aren't called to be pretty little birthday cake candles, or the ones people put around their bath before a good soak: we are called to be a light that is a fire which burns very brightly.

Sacred/secular

This sacred/secular divide has starved us from being able to practise resurrection to those who need it the most; we have written ourselves out of being the world's answer. If we are to be the movement Jesus intended, we need to re-find our feet as the centre of community and that is why we have a medical practice. Jesus healed so we, too, are practising healing.

We also have a project attached to the other church; this project houses teenagers who need somewhere to stay. It seeks to house those most at risk, such as single mums, and teens that have been kicked out of home because of their behaviour. A central aspect of this is that we seek to get them appropriate training before we find them a more permanent place to stay.

A central message for the Early Church was about redeeming humanity, and redeeming people's humanity. Everyone matters because everyone is made in that image of God. Naaman received his new humanity by being seen as clean again, the woman at the well received her humanity by no longer being an outcast. The children Sammy serves receive their humanity by being shown love and care – they become valued again. And the housing project gives back people's identity; they are no longer a person out on the street, but someone with a story that is worth hearing.

Powerless

I recognize that many of those that I work with think that they totally understand the world that they find themselves in. They behave like their today will be exactly like their yesterday. This is how the world worked on Tuesday therefore it will work the same on Wednesday. Many of those that I am working with say things like, 'Nothing seems to change!' and 'I don't want to have to keep going like this.'

Do you recognize this language?

So many people feel powerless to change their lives.

So many people feel powerless to kick a habit.

So many people feel powerless to rebuild a relationship.

So many people feel powerless to get out of debt.

So many people feel powerless to manage their time.

So many people feel powerless to find any contentment.

So many people feel powerless to escape reoccurring negative patterns of behaviour.

So many people feel powerless to see any hope.

So many people feel powerless to understand how life doesn't have to be this way.

More than social action, more than compassion

Now is the time for the church to be people of resurrection, to be people of a greater power, a greater rhythm. We were never designed to live life running on our own power; our Father put his breath inside of us. Our Father wants to help us, change us, and form us so that we are moving in his power so that we can administer the power to those who feel powerless.

What I am talking about here is more than social action. Many churches are involved in weekend serving programmes or, several times a year, litter clear-up projects or park sports projects. All this is good and is ultimately moving in the right direction, but there is a subtle difference between social action and being people of the resurrection.

There are many really good books looking at this idea of churches doing social action as a way of 'sharing the love of Jesus'. If we associate doing good works with mission then the ultimate reason for doing social action is to try to convert people to our faith. Jesus' resurrection brings life to the world as a *daily* event, not just on the third Saturday of the month when the church creeps out of its building to share the love of Jesus by painting fences. Jesus' resurrection needs to change the whole way that we see ourselves moving in the world.

Let me give you an example. Your church is involved in a small project on an estate doing litter picking, and you come across a young guy who is starving, he hasn't eaten for a while, so you give him a few quid to get some food. I would argue that the reason you give him a few quid is because you have compassion for him. You see that this is a young man who needs your help, so you give him what he needs. This is compassion.

Compassion isn't practising resurrection. If you were to practise resurrection in this situation you would give him the few quid he needs and you would then ask the question, 'Why is it he hasn't got any money to get food?' What is the reason for his need, what is the deeper need that he has? It might be that he's out of work; it might be that he is spending money on other substances, or he might be addicted to gambling. The resurrection gets us to ask the question, 'How do I bring life in abundance to this guy? Can I help find him work? Does he need support getting out of the repetitive circles his life is going in? Does he need help in being set free from addiction or something else that's holding him back?'

Compassion is when our heart feels sorry for someone or the situation, so we give a stopgap measure. True resurrection power sees the obvious need but then asks, 'What are the systems that are causing this need?' Resurrection is seeking justice for the young guy in whatever deeper need he has.

Spiritual acts and spiritual beings

So many Christians see their lives as separate and compartmentalized, living secularly on a Monday but spiritually on a Sunday, but this should not be the way we see ourselves. For Jesus, the whole of life was a spiritual act because we were created as spiritual beings. Practising resurrection is more than free cans of Coke, or litter picking, its about being people who have our eyes always open, looking to see where there is death, where there is a loss of humanity, where there is no longer hope and being the hope, life and resurrection.

Going back for a moment to the story of the Good Samaritan that we talked about earlier. The story is a prime example of people with their eyes shut and those with their eyes open. The two religious leaders' eyes were shut to the desperate need of the man who had been attacked. Their minds were upon the religious roles they were going to play at the Temple. They were thinking about readings, duties, preaching, worship leading, the children's work and the youth work. Their minds were upon what they were going to do; their minds were on being holy, righteous and good.

The Samaritan, on the other hand, had his eyes open to see what was happening in the world. He could see the man's pain, he could see his loss of humanity as he lay naked, and he could see he was at death's door.

When we are moving in the rhythm of the resurrection, our vision is centred upon people, because Jesus was centred upon people. The priest and Levite were looking inward, centred upon and caught up in their own religious activities and systems. These two religious men were caught up and in a rush because they had good, religious programmes to run in their church.

It is really important to note that what the two religious men were going to do was altogether worthwhile and biblical. They were following what God had told them to do, but they had a problem; they had missed that God himself was centred upon people – God was serving people. Practising resurrection was, and is, ultimate worship.

We make social action the limit to our practise of resurrection when we turn our good acts into evangelism and not into what they should be . . . worship.

Love God, love neighbour, love self

When Jesus was asked by one guy what he should do to inherit eternal life, Jesus responds by saying, '"Love the Lord your God with all your heart and with all your soul and with all your strength and with all your mind"; and, "Love your neighbour as yourself"' (Luke 10:27).

Love God and love the people.

For Jesus, the ultimate revelation of someone's heart was: could they love? Could they see outside their own religious ghetto, religious practises, their religious evangelism, and simply love people?

For Jesus, the way we can see the spiritual health of a church isn't about how much we sing worship, study Scripture or run amazing programmes. Jesus measures his global church – and therefore, us – on the way we serve those who are outside the church building.

In Matthew 25, Jesus unpacks this idea of our love for the broken. Practising resurrection for Jesus was ultimately there as a way for the world to see how broken lives can change in his resurrection. If you can show someone how a home can be transformed by someone spending a weekend painting it, then this is what Jesus' resurrection looks like in someone's own soul.

If an old man who hasn't had anyone visit him for fifteen years experiences the beauty of someone spending a short time showing him love by sitting and chatting, then this is a small representation of what Jesus' resurrection looks like in their soul.

If someone sees a broken and neglected section of land come to life as people repair and resurrect it with tender loving care, then this communicates what Jesus' resurrection looks like in the belly of their being.

Resurrection in the world reveals Jesus' resurrection in our own souls.

Love Jesus

Jesus sees people practising resurrection not only as a way of his resurrection restoring the world; he also sees it as something that we do to him. Jesus points out that our love for the world, which is practised on the least of this world, is ultimately done for him.

In Matthew 25:45, Jesus says that 'whatever you did not do for one of the least of these, you did not do for me.'

Practising resurrection on the least of this world not only impacts those we resurrect, it also affects our own relationship with Jesus, and our worship.

I don't want to talk much more on how practising resurrection is worship to Jesus; my point is that we can't see one-off social action projects as resurrection projects. Social action is a start of a much bigger resurrection process and is perfect for discipling and moving people to the point of wanting to be totally involved in resurrection. But social action in itself just isn't enough. It's hit and run. It leaves people wanting more, but we aren't there because we're back in our religious gatherings.

It's not about bums!

There is also a danger when we think that doing social action will get people into our worship gatherings; this isn't why we do it. The resurrection was never about bums on seats. We do it because we want people to connect with Jesus, and not our church. Yes, ultimately they may become fully committed members, but why we follow Jesus and practise his resurrection is a subtle difference to evangelism. We aren't about bums on seats, we're about being people who give life, and this life is so compelling and intriguing that others will want to be a part of this movement. But when it becomes merely about the movement, or our religious commun-ity and its numbers, we have ultimately lost the reason for existing.

We have to be so careful not to get dragged into subtly misunderstanding why we are church, why we are this Jesus movement. The danger is that gradually our purpose becomes about sin management and bums on seats rather than about resurrection life. We want to get people into a building to sort out their sin. Yes, Jesus did die for sin and its effects on the world, but this doesn't excuse us from making Jesus' resurrection movement only about trying to get them on a chair in our building so that we can tell them how they need to change their lives.

The true condition

Jesus was never about sitting people down to sort them out. He was about inviting them into a relationship where they could meet his resurrection power, spiritually and practically.

For Jesus, the way we love others displays the true condition of our hearts. If our love is about getting people into a church service, this isn't love. Neither is it love to tell them they're a sinner, convert them, and then leave them in the life they were living before – leaving them to sort out their own mess. The resurrection is about our sin, it's about our souls, it's about the cycles people fall into, and it's about resurrecting the whole of our lives.

And tears ran down her face

A little while ago, I was with a friend at a conference, speaking on the subject of practising resurrection. In one of the seminars, my friend Debs told this story about something that had happened to her.

As I jogged along one of my favourite places in Battersea Park, listening to Michael Jackson, and not feeling particularly holy or spiritual – actually, feeling the total opposite – I ran past a girl, maybe 30 or so years old, wearing a bright, and I mean bright, orange tracksuit. I heard a voice inside my head, saying, 'Go tell her that I love her and she shines brightly for me.' Dismissing this inconvenient voice I ran on, but to my dismay it came again "Go tell her that I love her and she shines so brightly for me.' Trying to practise obedience (Not sure if it was God, I thought it probably wasn't, but what did I have to lose?), I turned round and began to walk towards her, but got too scared and turned around in the opposite direction – only to hear the voice again. And so, finally, extremely embarrassed, I approached the woman in the tracksuit.

'I am sorry to bother you, but I am a Christian, and as I ran past you I just felt as though God wanted you to know that you shine brightly for him, and that he loves you. I don't normally do this, but I just wanted to tell you.'

Tears ran down her face as she began to explain her story to me.

She had just moved down from North London, and was living round the corner (I later discovered she had moved into the homeless unit with high support two minutes from my house), and this particular morning had decided to go for a walk, and was feeling low and lonely. She had stopped at the lake, and was praying, 'If there is a God, show me that you are real and that you have a plan for me being here.' As I jogged past, she prayed that I would stop and talk with her. She watched me run on and then stop and turn, and then stop and turn away again, at which point she prayed again that I would stop and chat and it was then that I turned round.

I, too, began to cry at this point. Partly out of shock – I hear that voice in my head the whole time, and are you telling me that that voice is God? I thought it was me, my thoughts, my ideas . . . !

We walked around the park and talked and exchanged numbers, and as we did, it was almost like I could see Jesus' resurrection power woven throughout our conversation. This was also the beginning of what has become a wonderful friendship. Amber had had a breakdown and spent time in hospital due to mental illness and attempted suicide. When she was finally discharged, she began to piece her life back together with the help of Jesus. She was housed in the secure unit in Battersea and started to live a better life. I have had the utter privilege of watching Amber venture along the path of life over those past few years as she has moved from a fragile and vulnerable woman to a confident lady who is taking life by storm. She found a good church where she has become a lay reader and has moved out of the secure unit into a home owned by the council, where she lives with others.

It was so real seeing the power of Jesus' resurrection working in her life, and it all started with me listening to God and turning around on that day. I never saw it as practising resurrection at the time, but this is totally what that day was.

I think what I found the most puzzling was that still, quiet voice was God, and that is such a familiar voice that I hear the whole time. It has made me realize that God is desperate to speak to me the whole time and desperate for people to know how much he loves them. I was feeling so unspiritual that day, it was such a boost to my faith as I again realized that God will use me whatever state I am in. What a beautiful thought.

The long pause

I stood in the classroom facing the question, had I ever raised someone from the dead? The response had to be yes; I've seen people with the messiest of lives come back to life as they have received Jesus' resurrection power.

I've seen young girls start as prostitutes and drug dealers, and watched them come back to life. I've seen young guys addicted to porn, with the weight of the world on their shoulders, standing with new life in their eyes. I've seen people with no hope – thinking the way their life has been means that's the way it's always going to be – realize there is a new hope for tomorrow. I've seen hope breathed into desperate situations, people coming free from their own lies, and I've seen unfair lives filled with joy.

Have I resurrected anyone? I've seen Jesus do a hell of a lot of resurrection.

The lesson ended and everyone rushed out, except three Muslim boys who stayed to ask more about 'this' Jesus.

Thinking deeper

- The problem in the sorry of Naaman was that the King had forgotten who he was and who he represented. Spend some time thinking about your faith. How does it affect the way you see yourself? Do you behave like a representative of the living God, or do you behave like it's a badge on your sleeve?
- Jesus sat with the woman at the well and brought her back to life by simply asking her for water. This simple act was done on a normal day in the midst of Jesus' journey. Where is your well, and who is fetching water? Is your well a coffee shop, bus or Tube line, corner shop or school gate?
- Who is your Samaritan? Is it a man or a woman? Is it someone who has a disability or someone with a different skin colour to you? Is it someone single or in a relationship? Is the person gay or straight? Is the person tattooed or pieced?
- Often our language communicates how we see people or how they see themselves. What language have you used in the past that has cast people out and made them distant?
- Who do you know that needs fresh, life-giving words spoken over them? What neighbour, friend or family member needs to be redefined as daughter or son? A virgin child?
- When we are moving in the rhythm of the resurrection, our vision is centred upon people, because Jesus was centred upon people. How have you seen your vision change as you have become more aware of Jesus' resurrection power?

Example of resurrection: Six

A real-life story about a person named Beth:

I knew I was missing out on something.

As I read my Bible, I found a Jesus who lived alongside and fostered intentional reciprocal relationships amongst the poor and marginalized. For Jesus, these people weren't a 'project' for him, they were his friends. I found Jesus' social circle deeply challenging as I read the Gospels and saw that his friends were the marginalized, the outcast and the sinners in society. And then I looked at my social circle – my friends were pretty similar to me; privileged, middle class and educated, a world away from those whom Jesus chose to spend his time with.

I knew I was missing out on something, but because my life was comfortable I was hesitant to do anything about it. I didn't want to replicate an arms-reach approach towards the poor, which only seemed to exaggerate the 'us' and 'them' chasm that already painfully exists. So, in an attempt to break out of our middle class, privileged, but often slightly dull, homogeneous bubble, some friends and I moved into the ninth floor of a deprived council estate in London.

I had been asking God where he wanted me to live and I felt him say, 'I want you to move onto a council estate and love people back to life.' God didn't tell me to go and begin projects, although projects can be good, or begin a charity, though charities can be good. He told me to go and just love people back to life. I was struck by the extreme loneliness that existed in these inner city high-rise tower blocks. It was Mother Teresa's wise words – that the greatest form of poverty is loneliness – that reverberated in my ears as I grappled with the command to practise resurrection amidst the deadening effect of unemployment, the dehumanizing welfare system and the allure of addictions making attractive but undeliverable promises.

In my naivety I thought many people's lives would change, and that there would be a re-enactment of Ezekiel in the valley of dry bones, each bone simultaneously coming alive and a large fleshly army assembling. I was sorely mistaken. I have instead learned that walking alongside those who are materially poor begins with befriending and loving one person, and it is in loving this one person that we are able to witness what Jesus meant when he declared that he came to bring life to the full. Jesus' encounter with the Samaritan woman radically demonstrates his compassion for the one person, as he broke both cultural and gender barriers, speaking with a woman who was stigmatized and marginalized in society. He sat down, engaged with, listened to, empowered, received from, and loved this one person back to life, rendering her irrevocably changed. I found this an outrageous and uncomfortable example to me. I have begun to realize that in reality, Ezekiel's transformation in the valley of dry bones happened one bone at a time. Jesus practised resurrection that day at the well. He breathed life and hope into the bones of the Samaritan woman.

Susan became the Samaritan woman in my life. She was a single mother, illiterate, severely depressed, on her fifth attempted suicide . . . but most importantly, she was my neighbour and became my greatest friend. Her depression had escalated due to her dark, dingy, undecorated flat, the broken bed that she was sharing with her teenage daughter, and repeated abuse from a previous partner. She existed but had never really lived life; she had spent her life in the grave clothes that Jesus told Lazarus to take off. Some friends and I offered to paint her kitchen and this is where our friendship began – over paint charts and endless cups of coffee, as we began the   mammoth

job of painting her entire flat. I watched her, cautious and scep-
tical at first, steeped in shame and embarrassment at her need
. . . there was no immediate life transformation, but ligament by
ligament, tendon by tendon, Susan came to trust and confide in
me as she, too, picked up a paintbrush and joined us in painting
her flat. After some months, she began to join us for pizza after
an evening of painting. The friendship grew. Her 15-year-old
daughter, however, was more of a challenge, as she would fre-
quently throw outrageous tantrums and refuse to talk to us –
which made her announcement even more surprising, when
she declared one day that she wanted to get baptized. (I was
astounded! There had been a large part of me that had even
wondered whether we were doing any good, and whether they
even realized that it was Christ's love that was our motivation.)

Apparently, our weekly painting sessions had had more effect
than I'd thought. We baptized Susan's daughter in the bath, a
beautiful and surreal sight, too many people squeezed into a
miniscule bathroom . . . but we did it.

Susan's dream was to travel abroad, but she had never
owned a passport and had only twice ventured outside
London. I was given two free first-class tickets to Paris, where
we went to celebrate her birthday, climbing the Eiffel Tower
and sailing down the River Seine – a day to remember for both
of us! Over these past five years, I have watched slow, often
snail's pace, change, but change nonetheless. As Susan
encountered hope for her life, as she has met Jesus and
received the riches of the kingdom, I watched her give out
some of what she had received as she helped organize and run
a community bus in the neighbourhood. The vision of the bus
was that it would be a place where our local neighbours could
come and receive a free manicure, be prayed for, drink coffee,
and experience the kingdom of God. Susan formed part of the
team, and each week she would make endless cups of coffee,
talk with and pray for all who came in. We wanted to create a

space where people could be loved back to life, to foster community, not isolation, to make people feel beautiful in a society wracked with low self-esteem.

Our unequal balance of friendship was readdressed as my life crumbled following the suicide of my best friend; as the tables turned, it was Susan who was the one who consoled me as I wept in her arms, and listened to me as I grappled to reconcile the resurrection power that Jesus offers in light of irreversible tragedy and loss. It was Susan who began phoning me, praying for me, and reminding me that the faithfulness and goodness of God was not dependent upon circumstances. As she saw me broken, vulnerable and real, our friendship deepened as she found that, as she had needed me, I now needed her. Reciprocity, a beautiful thing.

I experienced the mystery the apostle Paul talks about, of having nothing and yet possessing everything, of being poor, yet making others rich. Susan's life deeply enriched mine. Our background, education and life experience could not be more different, yet she is one of my greatest teachers and has become one of my greatest friends.

7.

Being the Answer to our Prayers

Lord, make me an instrument of your peace;
where there is hatred, let me sow love;
when there is injury, pardon;
where there is doubt, faith;
where there is despair, hope;
where there is darkness, light;
and where there is sadness, joy.
Grant that I may not so much seek
to be consoled as to console;
to be understood, as to understand,
to be loved as to love;
for it is in giving that we receive,
it is in pardoning that we are pardoned,
and it is in dying (to ourselves) that we are born to
    eternal life.

The Prayer of Francis of Assisi

Carrots, frames and gravestones

It was harvest time in the village church that I grew up in, and friends and I were having a band practise, surroun-ded by veg-etables and cans of food. The church was set out for the follow-ing day's harvest services and it looked great.

How it happened I no longer remember, but for some rea-son a large carrot had been thrown across the church past the communion table, past the organ, and had hit a huge picture clip frame and shattered the glass. The clip frame held images of the previous year's trip to Africa, but no longer any glass to protect them. We had the cunning idea that if we simply cleared away the remains of the glass then people may not notice it was gone. Glass is clear and so is no glass.

The glass wasn't put in a bin, as that would have been obvi-ous when they emptied the bin; the glass needed to be left somewhere no one would ever find it and link it to the crime. A friend of mine had a great idea where to put it, and decided not to tell us where it was. Then if we were ever asked, we could honestly say we didn't know where the glass had gone.

We arrived for the morning service and, as we arrived, one of the church leaders came straight to us and said, 'Good morning, boys! Any idea how the glass from the Africa clip frame ended up in the graveyard behind Mr Jones' grave? Mrs Jones visited the grave before the 8 a.m. service and found it hidden behind the stone. She also noticed the remnant of what looked like a glass-cut carrot. Any ideas?'

We all looked over at our friend. When he'd said he had a good hiding place, none of us thought this would be behind a grave. What a stupid place to hide the glass.

Anyway, without proof nothing could be proven so we denied everything.

Have you ever been the answer to someone's problem? Be it carrots and broken glass, or something far more serious?

Idiotsville

Mary grew up in south-west Galilee in a place called Nazareth. Nazareth was a small town during the time of Jesus, with only 160 to 200 people living in it. There is no mention of it in the Old Testament or in any other Jewish texts.

Galilee comes from the Hebrew word *galil* which translates as district, boundary or far territory. We might say out in the sticks. Galilee was the old country area away from the glitz of Jerusalem, the religious centre that was wealthy and powerful. The wealthy didn't live in Galilee, they left that area for the poor . . . with the worst area to live thought to be Nazareth.

Nazareth was considered by many as backward, a slow-moving town. It was seen as the place that the uncultured and unschooled lived; people from Nazareth were those who had no chance of success. Not only that, but it is also known that it was inhabited by Samaritans who had come in the hope of finding some work – Herod had been building not far to the west of Nazareth. This made Nazareth unclean and the place for the religious to avoid if at all possible. It had become a place of industry as the people used the resources available to them; although the rest of the nation looked down on them, they quietly worked hard to make life possible even though everyone else laughed at them.

To Jesus' friends, the term 'Jesus of Nazareth' was a friendly title, a title of affection, but to others it was a term of disrespect. This is why the Roman Empire had it put upon his cross. This was a term of put-down, like the phrase village idiot. Nazareth was where the thick idiots came from; Jesus was 'Jesus from Idiotsville'.

Can anything good come from Idiotsville?

In John 1:46, a man called Nathanael asked the question about Jesus' hometown, 'Can anything good come from Nazareth?'

This village Mary had been brought up in was the sticks, it was Idiotsville, it was the place nothing good could come from. This didn't stop the Roman Empire taxing the people of this small village as much as they could. People were struggling to make ends meet, life was tough and they hoped something would change. The dream was that one day a new king would come, like King David – a king who was about the people, a king who would be fair, just and loving; a king who would redeem the land of Israel and set the people free from the oppression of Herod and Caesar.

Mary probably dreamed and prayed about the day a saviour would come. Mary knew what it was like to be in a world of oppression and injustice, a world of prejudice and racism, and she prayed to God for his chosen Messiah to come and set it all right, bring *shalom*.

One day, when Mary is doing some normal, mid-afternoon, day to day task, an enormous messenger angel appears to her and tells her God has heard the cry of his people and has a rescue plan. God is to be birthed into the world where he is to move into the neighbourhood and become human. Then the angel says that God asks Mary to be the one who he breaks into the world through.

Imagine what was going through Mary's mind. She was still a virgin, probably only 13 or 14 years of age. People of the village would probably drag her out of the village and stone her for being so 'unholy' or 'unclean'. Mary would probably struggle to get her family's understanding on the matter and there was no chance a man would want to marry a woman who had been touched by another man. Everything in Mary would have said no to the offer.

Imagine living in the unclean village of the area that was already in the sticks and being the woman who would be stoned to death for being even more unclean. This would have made Mary the unclean of the unclean.

Bring it on!

Mary knows the situation and she also knows the desperation of the people. Mary could stay as the woman who prayed about the world's problems, or she could choose to be used by God not to just speak words of hope, but to *be* hope.

Mary stands in front of the angel and says, 'Bring it on! Let's get on with it.'

Mary wants not only to pray for an antidote, but is willing to *be* the antidote.

So Mary stands before this large messenger angel and says, 'Bring it on, let's do it!'

It was Sunday morning and I was the visiting speaker in a local church. It was almost my turn to stand up and teach that day's message, but just before that was the prayer time. Everyone sat quietly as an older lady stood behind the giant eagle, reading her well-crafted prayers. That morning we prayed for our church leaders, then the world leaders, before moving onto naming some of the issues found in our area:

> Lord, we pray for the homeless. Provide food and comfort for them as they sleep rough tonight. Lord, we also pray for the lonely. Would you give them hope and comfort as they sit at home alone? We also pray for those who are bought and sold into our country. May you help those who fight for their freedom.

The prayers were the typical Sunday church prayers, the usual prayers we have at my church too. The difference as I heard them this time was that I noticed one fundamental flaw in the prayers. These prayers asked God to do something but didn't asked God what he wanted us to do.

How can we pray for heaven to come to earth, as it says in the Lord's Prayer, but fail to see how we might be the very miracle needed for this to happen?

Mary stood in front of the huge messenger angel and realized she could just keep praying for the world to change, or she had an opportunity to be the answer to her prayers. Mary could cry out for the oppressed, but she also realized that she could be hope for the oppressed.

So Mary said, 'Bring it on.'

And Mary bust one out Snoop Dogg style

The moment the angel left her, Mary burst into what today would be a rap.

> I'm bursting with God-news;
>> I'm dancing the song of my Savior God.
> God took one good look at me, and look what happened–
>> I'm the most fortunate woman on earth!
> What God has done for me will never be forgotten,
>> the God whose very name is holy, set apart from all others.
> His mercy flows in wave after wave
>> on those who are in awe before him.
> He bared his arm and showed his strength,
>> scattered the bluffing braggarts.
> He knocked tyrants off their high horses,
>> pulled victims out of the mud.
> The starving poor sat down to a banquet;
>> the callous rich were left out in the cold.
> He embraced his chosen child, Israel;
>> he remembered and piled on the mercies, piled them high.
> It's exactly what he promised,
>> beginning with Abraham and right up to now.
>> *(Luke 1:46–55,* The Message*)*

Now they say 'Bring it on'

How often do we pray for the poor, the homeless or the widow, but don't realize that we might actually be the answer to our own prayers? We spend so long telling God the problems that we never listen to hear that God wants to send us to sort it out.

I recently spent some time serving in a homeless day care centre in Watford. During washing up, I got into a conversation with a girl about how she ended up working for the centre. Her story was long but ended with her saying that she had got fed up praying that people would sort out the homeless situation in the area. She realized that she could be a part of the solution.

Sometime later, I had another chat with a young guy giving a few weeks to the project. He said a similar thing, but in his story he had been leading prayers in his church for the homeless situation in his town and had found himself getting angry about how the local government weren't doing enough for those living in squats or on the streets. After he led the Sunday prayers, an older lady came up to him and said, 'So what are you going to do about it?' in the kind of way only an old lady can, probably adding a good 'young man' at the end. He had stood there for some time working out what to say before he realized his gut reaction was to say, 'Nothing. I'm just too busy.' But looking into her eyes, he knew his response had to be different; his prayers, his frustration left him needing to do something.

So he said, 'Bring it on.'

He made you

I was recently having coffee with a member of my church who was deeply frustrated with the way God, from his perspective, wasn't answering his prayers. We had gone through the different ways God responds to our needs, we had talked about God knowing what was the best for us, and how sometimes he knows better than us . . .! We had even talked about how God occasionally holds back to see how desperate we are to have something or see something change.

In a last chance of having a go at God, the guy argued, 'If God loved us so much, then why doesn't he answer our prayers about the poor? Is God really cruel enough to want to see how desperate I am to help someone in need?'

In a gentle response, I leaned forward and said, 'God did answer your prayers about the poor. He made you.'

The Early Church understood the situation, and they were becoming the answer to their cry. They, like Mary, knew what it was like to live in an occupied country with the oppressor breathing down their neck. They knew what it was like to be struggling financially, lacking in food and enough money to clothe themselves; they could see the world around them struggling to make it through the next week before the empire arrived again for taxes.

As mentioned earlier, in Acts 2 the church had this common pot that they all put their money into. People who were wealthy put in the money they raised from selling land and possessions, and the poor put in whatever they had, too. From this they then gave back what people needed, and out of what was left, they gave to the poor. The Early Church eradicated poverty – in Acts 4:34 it reads: 'There were no needy persons among them. For from time to time those who owned lands or houses sold them, [and] brought the money from the sales . . .' There was no needy person, poverty was eradicated.

One of the signs of the Holy Spirit coming at Pentecost was that poverty came to an end. This Early Church, this early Jesus movement, had learned what it meant to love one another and become the answer to their own prayers. They also recognized that it was a team effort. People were joining the team and wanted to join in practising resurrection; it was never about individuals, but a community. The early community didn't wait for Jesus to step in and practise resurrection; they as a community got on with it and did it themselves because he was in them. His Spirit was at work in them as a group of people out-working the resurrection, and we need to pray that we do the same thing.

Doing the stuff

Jesus is in the process of empowering us; he gives us the tools to be the answer to our prayers. He essentially invites us to join him in praying for the world – and then acting upon our frustrations, needs and longings for the world.

If this wasn't the case, then why did he instruct his disciples to do the stuff? He teaches them what to do, then sends them away to do it. Jesus isn't some divine CEO who keeps all the good work to himself while getting his underdogs to do the disillusioning jobs. Jesus trains, equips and then sends out in the Spirit.

Check out the story of the feeding of the 5,000. It is the disciples who come to Jesus, telling him there's a problem. It's getting late and people need feeding; they turn to Jesus to sort out the problem, and tell him to send the people away.

Jesus leans forward and tells them that the people are more than welcome to stay and that they, the disciples, need to solve the problem. Jesus knows that the disciples want him to send the people away so that they can have a night off, but he has other plans. Jesus gets the disciples to find some food from a little boy, blesses it and then they, the disciples, hand it out. The disciples become the answer to their own problem; they don't do it alone, but become the vehicle for God's intervention.

Jesus doesn't do experts

Jesus was always in the business of equipping and then inviting people to join his resurrection movement. The problem is that the church has, over time, turned Jesus into a cosmic vending machine which spits out all kinds of prayer solutions. We have turned God into yet another consumer choice; we pray to this God because we believe that he is the One who will be able to answer our prayers.

We have also moved into the rhythm of employing experts to do the work for us, under the disguise that we are unable to do the work due to lack of time or skill. Churches are employing evangelists so that members can bring their 'unsaved' to the expert to convert. We employ youth workers and then leave them to sort out the teens because they are the experts. We have generations of Christians growing up believing that there is two-tiered Christianity – the regular followers and the professional Christians.

Jesus wasn't in the business of equipping experts; he was in the business of equipping people to be disciples, followers and life-givers.

Imagine the faces of the disciples when they realized that they had to feed over 5,000 people on nothing but a bit of fish and bread. At their own hands, a miracle happened: they became the answer to their prayers.

Let me ask this question. Why would Jesus create more food when there is enough food to go around but the reason for the shortage is that the people just don't want to share? Would he create more food or does he invite people to change their hearts so that they become more caring, loving and giving? Does Jesus need to create more food, or does he ask us to use the third of the food the average Britain throws away each year in a better way?

Why would Jesus create more beds when there are homes with one or two spare, with some even being doubles? Does he invite us to make more or share what we have?

The risk

When you create a world like this, you always have the risk that the people you create aren't willing to govern or run it in the way you want them to. So you have two options: Run it like a dictator, where you stand over   people telling them how they should behave – which tends to make people hate you or despise your authority; or, sit back and invite people to become the people you created them to be – inviting them into a movement that allows people to live good, empowering lives. And then, when you see someone choosing to live your way, a good way, this makes you feel proud, overjoyed and satisfied.

We have a couple who are members of our church. A few years ago, they were visiting a family they knew who lived abroad. When they were there, they could see that the family wasn't a healthy one – the father had been abusing the mother and she no longer had what she needed to care for the family. The children were having to do more and more to care for themselves and they themselves were being emotionally bullied by their dad. Things had to change, the family needed to break free from the over-oppressive father, and it had to happen soon.

The children and the mother were scared because no one knew what the father would do next. Praying quickly on the spur of the moment, the visiting couple knew that they had to do something. They couldn't just leave the place asking God to do something, they needed to pray and be the answer to their prayers in the same time.

The evening ended with them in the back of a police car with the mother and children and a small packed bag. Days later, the mother was getting long-term support from extended family and the children were back in the UK with the couple.

When they talk about what happened that night, all they can say is, 'We had to do something, we couldn't do nothing.' The reality was that they *could* have done nothing, they could have walked away praying that somehow God would intervene and rectify the situation. Yet they knew they needed to pray and be the answer with Jesus' resurrection power.

How can we sit back and pray for the oppressed when we could be the answer to their prayer – we could be the answer to *our* prayer?

Jesus had an assumption

Jesus' prayers always assume that he is going to be in some way a part of the answer.

There is some role for Jesus to play in the ongoing work of death to life. On the night of Jesus' betrayal, the day before his execution, he is fully aware of the direction this is going in, and he is praying in the garden, and this prayer reveals how he sees his part is to be played out. In Mark 14:35 it tells us that Jesus falls to his knees and prays, 'If this is possible, make this hour pass from me.' Jesus asks if it's possible to do it another way, use some other means to rectify the problem, use someone else.

Jesus goes on to pray further, 'If this isn't possible . . . yet not what I will, but what you will.' The first part of the prayer is Jesus asking for a way out, some other way for this night to pan out, but then he prays, 'If it's going to go this way, if this hour is coming, then I'm in if it's your will.'

Jesus knows that if this has to happen, then may it be in the way that God wants it to go. Jesus knows that he has a part to play and that he is in his Father's hands, this is his Father's work, and he is playing his redemptive part.

If it has to go any way, Jesus wants it to go his Father's; Jesus makes it clear that he knows this direction is going to cost him dearly but his response shows his commitment – 'Bring it on.'

Driving away with teenagers and a mother in the back of the police car, the couple could have simply prayed, and maybe God would have done something. But they knew that if God wanted to do something and this cup could not be passed from them, then they needed to say, 'Bring it on.' And their response was to say they couldn't have done anything else. They had to play their part in this redemptive event, they had to set this family free and they had to practise resurrection.

Super or natural

This isn't to undermine supernatural intervention; God is always at work and he is supernaturally answering prayers in ways that we can't ever comprehend. I personally have experienced supernatural healing. I have seen it in those that I have prayed with, I could tell you story after story of people I personally know that have been healed by God supernaturally. I believe in his intervention, but I also believe that there have been times in history where some forms of Christianity have used this as an excuse for doing nothing. It's like their over-spiritualizing makes them apathetic about getting their hands dirty. We need to *pray* for divine intervention, and we need to *act* like nothing else matters. The answer is both. Jesus ministered supernatur-ally and he ministered naturally. The feeding of the 5,000 only happened because the disciples were willing servants and because God acted supernaturally – the answer is both.

So if there is a problem is the answer a natural or a supernatural one?

I believe the answer is yes!

If someone I was working with was homeless, to only pray for them and not to try to give them any actual help would be doing them a great injustice. But if I gave them food and a place to sleep but never prayed for them, I would be guilty of the same thing. Justice, compassion, serving and loving is both super and natural. We serve through our relationship with Jesus, and we pray for his Spirit to be at work.

The answer is a resounding YES.

Choosing to need us

The question that we should be asking is 'What is God up to, what is he doing, and how can we be involved?' Because it's the super and the natural, we need to work in his rhythm, in his ministry.

Some people I know will say this is absurd; we can't be the answer to our prayers because God is the only answer to our prayers. He is the only One who can correctly step in and make a fundamental difference. But I would argue that there is this amazing reality that there is a God who ultimately chooses to use us. God wants to see the world changed – we know this because of his Son, Jesus – but he doesn't want to do it without us. He wants to feed the 5,000, but he wants to do it through his people. God wants to partner with us in reclaiming the world; he wants to partner with his creation in reworking and redeeming the creation.

This is the beauty of the God of love.

Well-intentioned rock stars

The danger with this is that we can start to see ourselves as the saviour, as the redemptive power in the work, and this is how empires and kingdoms are built. We see this sometimes when an international speaker or someone in the centre of a huge move of the Spirit starts to see themselves as not only the answer, but also the one who is the power behind the answer.

We aren't God, neither are our leaders, and neither are well-intentioned rock stars.

It is so important to realize that we can never be the answer to our prayers without God. It reads in 1 John 4:12 that 'if we love one another, God lives in us'. The answer is God working through us; we aren't the saviour, but the Saviour is in us.

This is God at his funniest. The God who created the universe, called it into being, is the same God who chooses to use us. Moses the stuttering shepherd becomes the voice of God, a barren woman gives birth to a new nation, a small insignificant shepherd boy becomes the greatest king, and the little homeless refugee child born in a stable leads   people home.

Prostitutes and murder – in no particular order

God has never been afraid of our faults and failings, and he hasn't ever been worried about using them to work his resurrection power. In Matthew 1 we read a genealogy starting from Abraham right through to Jesus. This line passes through several interesting stories, that of Tamar, Rahab, Ruth and Uriah's wife, Bathsheba. All these stories are messy: Tamar and Rahab are prostitutes; Ruth was remarried to Boaz and wasn't even Jewish; then there's the story of David's illegitimate sex with Bath-sheba, and the murder of her husband.

God uses the messy lives to paint his picture. God isn't into the clean-cut story and never shies away from the reality of life. He is just looking for people who will join Mary in saying, 'Bring it on.'

This is the paradox of a holy God who chooses to use us: damaged, frail and with all our shortcomings.

He chooses to need both you and me.

Calcutta

Mother Teresa knew what it was to be the answer to her prayers; she spent years serving the poor in Calcutta with the hope of bringing Jesus' resurrection to those in so much desperation. Every day she is said to have used this prayer as a way of centring herself before she served those in need.

Dear Jesus, help us to spread your fragrance everywhere
　　we go.
Flood our souls with your spirit and life.
Penetrate and possess our whole being so utterly that
　　our lives may only be a radiance of yours.
Shine through us, and be so in us, that every soul we
　　come in contact with may feel your presence in our soul.
Let them look up and see no longer us but only Jesus!
Stay with us, and then we shall begin to shine as you shine;
　　so to shine as to be a light to others; the light O Jesus, will
　　be all from you, none of it will be ours; it will be you,
　　shining on others through us.
Let us thus praise you in the way you love best by
　　shining on those around us.
Let us preach you without preaching, not by words but
　　by our example,
by the catching force, the sympathetic influence of what we do.
The evident fullness of the love our hearts bear to you.
Amen

Thinking deeper

- Mary stood in front of the angel and said, 'Bring it on.' Who have you seen respond to God in the same way? Has there been someone that you have been inspired by because of their willingness to be used by God?
- If someone asked you to potentially wreck your life in the hope that your sacrifice would birth something new, would you be willing to be involved?
- How do you need to respond to Jesus' call as Mary did on your own life?
- How does it make you feel, thinking that you have more than you need while others have less? Do you have any-thing spare which could be shared around?
- Read the story of the feeding of the 5,000 found in Matthew 14:13–21. Read it slowly and reflect on what Jesus does and what the disciples do. Jesus could have done this miracle on his own but chooses not to. Why do you think this is?
- What real need could you be being asked to respond to with the help of Jesus' miraculous power?
- To respond to this chapter you might like to turn back to the beginning of it and reread through The Prayer of Francis of Assisi. You could print it out and put it on your door so that as you daily leave your home, you have a reminder that you are called to be an instrument of peace.

Example of Resurrection: Seven

A real-life story about a project called Maseno:

Maseno is located in the heart of Kenya in a very poor region. The area is noticeable for all the drunkards and orphans walking the streets, and the amazing African heat. This is a story of how the resurrection power is at work in such an area.

HIV has been a growing problem in Africa for some time. Because of the lack of work, the men have been migrating into the cities trying to find employment. This migration means that many of the men are parted from their wives and children, who remain on the farms trying to keep the *shamba* (farm) running. Being away from home and being able to live a much more anonymous lifestyle results in the men becoming tempted to live a more sexually promiscuous lifestyle while succumbing to the pleasures of the city life.

These originally farming men acquired HIV in the cities and then brought it back to the families. Over time, whole families have become riddled with the virus and whole generations have died because of it. Many men have died and not passed on any farming techniques to their wives or children; this means now most farms in the area aren't producing what their land ought to produce if used well.

In 2004 Revd Bruce Collins, a church leader from London, visited the area and discovered that the depth of the poverty found in the Maseno area was perpetuated by the lack of farming knowledge in the local population. This broke his heart and soon broke the heart of many Christians back home. For generations, many families have farmed these smallholdings in Maseno without success and without the necessary knowledge, leading to hunger and poverty within one of the most fertile areas of Kenya.

It was from this that the Maseno Farm School Project was formed in the belief that caring for widows and orphans was a direct requirement of the Christian faith. Local people were brought on board who had previous farming knowledge, and knowledge of buying seed and fertilizers.

In 2005, a team went out from Harrow, London with the specific purpose of dreaming and creatively seeing what could be done without it ever becoming a simple aid project. This project had to be sustainable; it had to help the farmers help themselves.

The Maseno project was set up as an agricultural project that would help the farmers there to become self-sufficient after a period of three to four years. The intention was to establish a model that could be replicated easily in other areas within Kenya and beyond.

After asking the local farmers (who are both male and female) about the problems that they faced, it was discovered that if they ever had any excess produce to sell at a large town or city market, they had to set off as early as 3 a.m. and walk up to eight miles carrying the produce for sale – or, if they were lucky, carrying their goods on a bicycle. If they did not sell the produce, they had to then carry the goods all the way back to their homes.

The project needed to train the farmers to produce better crops and then help them to sell what they had without having to travel a day to do so.

Five years on, the project now has twenty-one farm schools, with each school training around thirty farmers. Each farm school buys or rents a plot of land as a demonstration plot. On these plots each school is able to grow crops under controlled conditions, and the farming students are able to measure and gauge the results, thereby giving practical examples of crop growth and success or failure in differing techniques.

Each farm school also elects a chairman and a facilitator, which gives responsibility for the success of each school to the local population rather than this being imposed by outsiders. Each farm school is subsidized on a decreasing scale for a period of three years. Bringing relief from poverty through education is the main aim of the Trust.

Farmers are encouraged to give a tithe of 10 per cent to the community storehouse from the crops of maize and vegetables that they produce. This tithe is used to feed orphans, buy more seed and fertilizers, and to give a small amount to the church for its work. Within the small area that the project originally started are seven orphan feeding programmes, each feeding around one hundred to one hundred and fifty orphans. The Maseno project is now helping to feed the farmers, giving them enough to tithe and enough to sell through the project, but is also feeding those most in need.

Through teaching and education, the project aims to bring empowerment, self-sufficiency and a sense of community and trust between people and different tribes. The whole programme means that eventually this region will not have to rely upon continuous, ongoing, long-term aid from the wealthier Western world, but rather the local community will become self-supporting.

A typical short rain season would originally produce two bags of maize. Now it's producing as much as eight bags per farmer. Poverty is being eradicated and the resurrection is being seen so powerfully. Lives are being transformed because people were willing to use their gifts and skill, people were willing to be broken and poured out.

One single mother, who is also a farmer, graduated from the farm school and cried because in the last three years she has seen her life turned around and is now able to provide for her family.

There is one woman who three years ago described herself as a widow. She now describes herself as a successful businesswoman.

There is one man who was feeding his cow almost all he had to try and get some milk for his family. He has now been shown how to feed his livestock, and has thereby increased his milk yield by 80 per cent.

Lives are being changed in Maseno. Not because the *masungoo* (white man) has gone there and given money, but because people have given up resources and time to train people in more productive ways of farming.

8.

Prophets and Kings

Never doubt that a small group of thoughtful,
committed citizens can change the world.
Indeed, it is the only thing that ever has.

Margaret Mead, twentieth-century anthropologist

A long line of messiahs

Jesus isn't the only person to have been called the Messiah. The name Messiah comes from the Hebrew meaning Anointed One, which in the Greek is translated as Christ. Before Jesus arrived on the scene there had been many other people who the Jews had called the Messiah, and post-Jesus there were other significant possibilities.

In the Catholic Bible there is a section of stories found between the Old and New Testaments, called the Apocrypha. These stories are sometimes extended mythical stories, and other times are historical accounts of the events between the Old Testament and the birth of Jesus. There is one story found in the book called the Maccabees which talks of God's people coming back to Jerusalem and specifically how this happened through a man called Judas Maccabeus.

I was chatting to a Jewish neighbour of a friend of mine, and we got talking about Hebrew Bible heroes. He mentioned that his was Judas Maccabeus, who many of us will not have heard of, but to Jewish people this is a name well known.

Judas Maccabeus is held as one of the greatest warriors of the Jewish faith alongside King David. He lived around two hundred years before Jesus, and became known as a messiah. Judas Mac (as we will call him) reclaimed the city of Jerusalem from the Greeks and restored the services in the Temple. This reconsecration of the Temple is still celebrated today as a Jewish holiday called Hanukkah.

The Jewish faith has always been looking for a Messiah who it is believed will do three things: Liberate God's people from exile, bring a return to a YHVH-centred rule, and restore the Temple for worship.

In the book of Maccabees, Judas Mac did all of these so he was known and called the Anointed One or Messiah. There are others in the Bible who are also known as a messiah; King

David was known as the Anointed One, the Messiah, the one who brought the people together into freedom. He put YHVH in the centre of society and he, too, started to design the Temple for God.

The Messiah job

But what is the point of this random bit of history for us today? For the Jews, the Messiah's job wasn't to offer a ticket to some kind of eternal celebration with God, or the promise of eternal life and the knowledge of a better place; the Messiah's job was to bring a real-life global reign of peace here on earth, to change life and bring quality of life. This was known as *shalom*, which we looked at earlier – being whole, connected, integrated, as well as about quality of life, nothing missing, nothing broken, well-being, complete, justice, prosperity and health.

This was the job of the Messiah, to bring *shalom*. All the other messiahs only did it for a short period of time; soon someone else would come and destroy what they had built. But Jesus came as the one Ultimate Anointed One, the true Messiah, the true Christ. In Matthew 16 we see that Peter understood that this was the role of the Messiah – that's why, when Jesus asks him who he thinks he is, he replies, 'the Messiah'. Jesus goes on to say in the conversation that he is going to die, to which Peter's response is that this is impossible. They needed a Messiah who would liberate and fight for the people, and whilst Peter understood the role of the Messiah, he'd only ever seen or expected this to be played out in the lives of an earthy Messiah who tried to do it by force. When Peter tries to stop Jesus from suffering and dying, Jesus shouts, 'Get behind me, Satan!' This response from Jesus has baffled many in the church for years. The reality was that Jesus wasn't going to be the kind of Messiah that the Jewish people had seen before or were expecting.

Jesus' idea was that he would suffer and die by serving and surrendering, and this was a totally new and revolutionary concept.

Chocolate heaven and Umpa Lumpa angels

In the last 2,000 years we have turned Jesus' idea of being the liberator, the Messiah, into a Willy Wonka theology. Faith has become about getting our golden ticket so that we have a space booked on the trip to chocolate heaven where it will be perfect as we sit and drink from the chocolate stream of life. I guess in this line of theology the angels become Umpa Lumpas and the pearly gates become made of candy canes.

Christianity in the last 2,000 years has become about longing and waiting for the day we get to use our golden ticket to get into those pearly candycane gates. When we have this idea of Christianity, the faith becomes about being saved from our sin and then sitting back, getting comfortable, and watching the world go by until we arrive.

This Willy Wonka theology is turning the church into an unappetizing product that no one is interested in. People want to see a Jesus that changes their lives today and not just when they die.

I was speaking at a youth conference some time ago about this idea of Willy Wonka heaven. I spoke about how Jesus wasn't looking for people to join him in heaven, but that he was looking for people to join him in bringing heaven to earth, right here, right now. As I was speaking, a young man appeared on the right of the stage and approached me. I have to admit I thought he was coming to grab me for being a heretic or give me a good kicking. He didn't look like the kind of guy that wanted to hug me. As he approached, I noticed a gold card in his hand. He handed it to me and, in shock, I started to read the text printed on it. It read:

> Congratulations on becoming a follower of Jesus. He is preparing you a room in eternity as we speak and it is going to be perfect for you. This ticket is non-transferable.

We have made Christianity a product that only comes into play the moment we die, and nothing is further from the truth. The role of the Messiah was to liberate us from our own slavery, bring God back to the centre of our reality, and to bring us *shalom* on every level of our lives.

No wonder young people leave the church every week when we have made Jesus about longing and waiting. Teenagers hate waiting.

Jesus Christ, the Anointed One, came to bring liberation today, right here, right now.

Polis

Jesus was interested in all the complicated bits of life, not just where we relax after we are dead. Sadly, Christianity has made Jesus into nothing more than a glorified preacher when in reality he was a politician and legislator who was interested in the reality of today. The word politician comes from the Greek word *polis* meaning city, or the affairs of the city. Much of Jesus' teaching had a political slant; we have already seen this in many of his stories, we clearly see this in his street performance whilst riding a donkey into Jerusalem, and we see it in his willingness to die at the hands of the empire.

A politician is ideally someone who cares about the affairs of the community, they care about people, and they care about *shalom* on every level of society.

Like our Messiah Jesus, we need to follow in his footsteps and be politicians; we need to care about the affairs of our community, right from birth to death, teenage pregnancy to elderly care. We need to practise resurrection in our communities; we can't leave politics to the politicians, we need to be involved with the ground-level working of our governments. This is why my church chose to be involved in policymaking regarding bullying in our area. We help speak into what our council do with regard to caring for the young people who are being bullied.

Every gathered resurrection community needs to be involved in speaking resurrection life into every level of society. We are in a dangerous position when we become about gathering to worship, forgetting to engage with the world around us. There is a danger that we make the 'spiritual' more important than the 'secular', when in fact they are deeply intertwined.

Prophets

I imagine Samuel the prophet to be a wise old man with a staff and sandals, a little like Gandalf in *The Lord of the Rings*, someone with real depth and authority but still alive with energy. Samuel was the one who had the privilege of anointing Saul to be king of Israel, but not long after Samuel also had to rebuke Saul for not keeping the commands God had given him.

Later in Israel's story, the King was David and he, too, had a prophet lingering around him. Nathan the prophet went to David to tell him to hold back on building God his Temple; he also had to go to David to rebuke him for his affair with Bathsheba.

Elijah the prophet directed King Ahab, Daniel spoke to and directed King Nebuchadnezzar, and then in the Gospels, John the prophet shouted at King Herod.

Often when we see a king we see, too, a prophet directing and declaring a word from God. Sometimes this relationship is a positive one, and sometimes it's a difficult and tense relationship.

The prophets were always in relationship to the king in some way, they always had access to the king, but they were never controlled by the king or worked for the king. The prophets were there to march to the beat of God, speaking his legislation and law, and never to allow the kings to draw them away from their fundamental understanding of *shalom*.

When we live with Willy Wonka theology there is no reason why we shouldn't let kings get away with their bad behaviour. People who live with this theology say things like 'one day we will be with our true King and things will be different, so let's just endure this life for the moment' or 'God will make things better in the end'.

Passing on through

I had a Christian recently tell me that there was no point caring for the environment because one day Jesus would come and redeem it anyway. This is a guy who knows Jesus' resurrection life, he has seen it working in him, but he still sees this world as a place he will leave. This friend is an environmental scientist and knows all about weather patterns and how the environment is affected by human behaviour. He sees the world in a mess and doesn't see this as a problem because God will destroy and rebuild it.

While walking to work the other day I passed a car with a bumper sticker that read 'This is not my home, I'm just passing through'. This isn't a new bumper sticker and I have seen the same message on posters in church offices around the country. What is it that this bumper sticker is saying? Could it be that while trying to communicate a message that there is another life to be lived after this life, it in fact communicates a message that this world is not important because I have a better place to go when I die? Or not so mildly putting it: Who gives a stuff about this world and all of you stuck here, because I'm going to be going somewhere better! Could it be that we as Christians have focused so much on converting people, and church roof projects, that we have in fact missed a major command back in Genesis?

Dressing and blessing

It says in Genesis 1 that *Elohim* created the heavens and the earth in six days and he said it was 'good'. The word good communicates that the world wasn't 'perfect' (as in complete) because that would indicate that the work was finished. When something is perfect it doesn't need any more work. Good indicates that there is going to be an ongoing work making this thing better. Good reveals that it was never perfect and that God expected it to grow and change with age, and because of this, in Genesis 2:15 *Elohim* commands humankind to look after it. *Elohim* 'took the man and put him in the Garden of Eden to work it and take care of it.'

The word work is the Hebrew word *ovd* which can also be translated as to serve, and to dress, in the sense of making presentable, like a servant would serve and dress his master. The word care is the Hebrew word *shomr* which can be translated as keep, preserve, protect, watch, bring justice to or speak out for in a similar way to that of a prophet.

A good analogy of what God is communicating here is that of a baby. The baby can't feed itself or wash itself, neither can it dress itself, the baby needs 24/7 care with someone looking over it constantly. The baby can't protect itself or stand up for itself and, on occasions, may need someone to speak out and bring justice for it, as it has no voice of its own. Prophets speak out for those who don't have a voice, they give a voice to the speechless, but they also give a voice to God's kingdom.

In essence, God is calling humankind to serve the earth and dress it in the same way we would do with a young baby. The earth cannot care for or bring justice to itself. It is powerless and this is why God calls Adam to do this work.

Which means that right at the dawn of time, *Elohim* commissioned humankind to be the parent, representative or prophet to the whole of creation. Which means that we need to be aware of the way we interact with creation. Do you give any thought to the products you buy? How much energy has been wasted in making this product and its packaging? What did it cost the environment in flying it or bringing it by boat to your local store? There isn't just the cost of buying the product we have to be aware of; we need to be aware, too, of the greater cost to the world. Every bit of energy used to power machines and vehicles produces carbon dioxide, which raises the amount of greenhouse gases created.

God has called us to be prophets for the whole of creation, to speak out, to dress and protect.

Coffee cup 230

For some time now, Starbucks have printed little quotes on their takeaway cups under the title of 'The way I see it'. Cup number 230 reads:

> Heaven is totally overrated. It seems boring. Clouds, listening to people playing the harp. It should be somewhere you can't wait to go, like a luxury hotel. Maybe blue skies and soft music were enough to keep people in line in the 17th century, but heaven has to step it up a bit. They're basically getting by because they only have to be better than Hell

Has coffee cup 230 not read Revelation 21? Obviously not!

The Gospels never paint a picture of life after death, dwelling on some distant cloud or land beyond this planet. The Bible never paints the picture of pearly gates and St Peter waiting to log you in or out.

Many people have the idea that the plan is to break out of this place into a better world, but the Bible claims that it will be heaven crashing into this world. Revelation 21 paints a picture of a new earth coming out of the sky to renew and rebuild this earth. Revelation 21 is about everything finding its proper place here, broken things beautifully re-pieced together in vibrant harmony. This verse goes on to read that the former things will pass away, or depart. Revelation 21:1 says the *protos* (former), things *apelthan* (depart). *Protos* is the first things or the prototype things – the things that are sinful (*chatta't*) that come from the Garden of Eden. *Apelthan* is a wonderful word that for me is understood more in the image of a potter moulding out all the creases and lines in the pot that he is making; in the same way, God will mould out the dints and lines in his creation. When it reads that the former things depart from this creation, this is the image of the Creator God, reworking his creation. Revelation 21 then claims that this earth will become the heaven we will live in for eternity. It was never about us going to God but about a God coming to us.

When we have a theology that says this place is not our home but we are just passing through it communicates to those living around us that this earth has no value to Christians. If we were to read the Lord's Prayer in Matthew 6 we find it says, 'your kingdom come, your will be done on earth as it is in heaven.' The Lord's Prayer speaks of God's kingdom in heaven becoming a reality here on earth. Another word for kingdom is the word government. This speaks of a locality being ruled and governed by a certain power, and that this power will be coming here to change the way this world works.

Metaioteti

It says in Romans 8:20 that 'the creation was subjected to frustration', the word in the Greek here which we translate as frustration is the word *metaioteti* which could also be translated as brokenness and frailty. So in other words creation is broken, and later in verse 22 it says that the creation, alongside us, is waiting to be liberated from the bondage of death. The interesting nugget of this text is that it tells us who is going to play a part in this liberation of the earth; it says back in verse 19 that 'creation waits in eager expectation for the sons of God to be revealed.' The text says 'sons', as in plural not singular making it clear that it's not just Jesus the earth is waiting for. Who are the sons? The sons are God's children who are going to play their part in restoring the earth with Jesus. We are people of Jesus' resurrection who are to therefore bring resurrection not only to other humans, but also to a broken, damaged world.

The prophets engaged with the kings because they were passionate about the affairs of the whole of life. They knew there were no spiritual and physical distinctions, and David writes in Psalm 24 that 'the earth is the LORD's, and everything in it' (v. 1).

This bold statement appears many times in my mind when prepping for my day to day workload. It has helped me frame some of my thoughts about God's kingdom work within the communities we live.

'The earth is the Lord's, and everything in it', which is also found in 1 Corinthians 10, requires us to engage with culture for the cause of Jesus' resurrection gospel. The prophets were always speaking of an alternative reality not only to the kings, but also into the hopelessness and despair that they found in those around them.

They were prophets to the kings, but also prophets to the people.

As we approach our communities like the prophets approached theirs, we need to believe in that different narrative being worked out in the world through Jesus' hands and feet; a different story being worked out by Jesus' resurrection community. We need to believe in a Messiah who is always at work because his Father is always at work and that this Messiah is always at work through us; his church. We as prophets will be the expression of God's kingdom in our communities, speaking truth, mercy, love and power. The Body of Christ revealing Christ, making him tangible to the people he loves.

Christianity isn't about a warm fuzzy feeling. It is about giving us a heavenly perspective of this world, in this reality. Jesus didn't do what he did on the cross so that we might go to church, but that we might change our nation.

We are called to be prophets. We are called to speak God's agenda, God's legislation for the poor, the oppressed, the bewildered and the abandoned. And to speak it to whoever we have the power to reach.

God's arena – our arena

When the whole of life is God's arena, we need to make the whole of life our arena, or at least make sure that the church covers every area. We can't all be involved in every little bit of our community but there is a danger when there are whole chunks of our community that aren't being influenced by God's grace. The resurrection community needs to be involved in all areas. Every aspect of life should be invaded by God. The problem is that the church hasn't engaged for so long in some of these areas that whole generations haven't seen what the resurrection community is capable of.

We need to stop seeing one thing as secular and normal and another as sacred and holy, and we need to see the whole of life as the arena that God's prophets must speak into.

Paul wrote to the new church in Ephesus that '[God's] intent was that now, through the church, the manifold wisdom of God should be made known to the rulers and authorities' (Eph. 3:10). It was God's intent that his people would speak directly into the politics of the time; God's wisdom being made known to the rulers and authorities.

Moses the prophet

Egypt had dehumanized God's people; they had turned them into slaves – people who could build their kingdom on the cheap. Builders, plumbers and architects were all forced to build Egypt's empire by the power of the whip.

This was an Egyptian sweatshop with workers of all ages, children, elderly, men, women, all being forced to make bricks and build towers. No one was left out of this oppressive regime.

So here we have a man called Moses who spoke with a stutter (Exod. 4:10). Moses wasn't the kind of man who could articulate himself well, but he was a man who had seen the reality of the world of Egypt, and a man who had had a sense of right and wrong from a young age. We read in Exodus 1:11 that Moses saw an Egyptian beating a Hebrew to make them work harder. Moses, feeling angry about what he saw, grabbed and killed the man. Moses knew that the oppression of God's people was evil but he didn't know how to deal with it.

God called this unlikely hero to be a prophet, to be his voice for the oppressed. God didn't look at Moses' ability, but he honoured his availability and saw his potential. God sent Moses to speak to Pharaoh, each time showing a sign of God's power.

I don't know what you think about the ten big plagues that God used to hit Egypt in the Exodus story. Often God ends up looking like a cruel and nasty deity. But what if those plagues were more subtly making a statement about who God was? What if they were proving that YHVH was not a god, but *the* God?

During the time of the Exodus story, the people of God found themselves being oppressed by the Egyptians and, more specifically, the pharaoh. The Egyptians worshipped a large selection of gods at this time, with one or two being the major gods. I would argue that these plagues were there to show how the Egyptian gods were in fact not gods at all, but that YHVH was the God.

Let's look at some of these gods for a moment. The god Hapi was the god of the River Nile or, more precisely, the Nile was a god. It was believed that this god made the land fertile. Once a year the Nile would flood into the fields, allowing crops to grow.

The goddess Hekt was the frog-headed goddess. It was said that this goddess played a part in the creation of the world and was still in the process of creating every spring.

There was a god called Geb who was known as the god of the earth, who was able to make things from the dust of the earth.

The god Khephera, the fly god, and was linked with bravery. There was a story of a fly flying inside people to see their hearts, to see what their hearts were made of.

The goddess Hathor was the cow-headed goddess of animals, who was linked to love and romance.

The god Im-Hotep was thought to be the god of healing. The Egyptians would bring offerings to Im-Hotep to be made well again.

The goddess called Nut was the mother of the sun-god Amon-Ra and was called 'The sky goddess' who was thought to allow things of the sky to happen. Rain, sun, hail, thunder. (It wasn't that she made these things, but allowed them to occur.)

Senehem was the locust-headed god and was linked to anger.

The god Amon-Ra was the sun god and was the principal deity of the Egyptian gods.

And then Pharaoh was thought to be the supreme god of Egypt, with Pharaoh's son being the supreme god of Egypt to be.

One by one, YHVH sends his plagues to show who really is in charge. YHVH turns the Nile into blood, which was a sign of this god being dead and no longer having any ability to bring fertility to the fields.

God shows he is greater than the frog goddess Hekt, and Geb, by showing his creative ability by bringing to birth thousands of frogs and by creating the gnats from the dust. He is also a creative God.

God then creates thousands of flies that too become pests, but also could be seen to be showing how YHVH can see everything by being everywhere, like the flies. God then kills all the livestock showing how he has control of the animals, not Hathor. God then sends the plague of boils upon the Egyptian people. At which point, the people would have gone into the temple of Im-Hotep for healing, giving their sacrifices, but we can presume healing didn't occur, showing that YHVH is Almighty.

Then, before he finishes, YHVH proves his power by making it hail, proving the Nut goddess of the sky could not stop him; he then sends thousands of locusts making Senehem look like a pest, and blots out the power of Amon-Ra by bringing darkness upon the land.

God then finishes by showing he is Almighty by breaking the chain of pharaohs by killing the Pharaoh's son, showing that the pharaohs are nothing but human, and not divine.

Pharaoh should have known better right at the start of the story when in Exodus 7:10–12 it says that 'Moses and Aaron went to Pharaoh and did just as [YHVH] commanded. Aaron threw his staff down in front of Pharaoh and his officials, and it became a snake. Pharaoh then summoned wise men and sorcerers, and the Egyptian magicians also did the same things by their secret arts: Each one threw down his staff and it became a snake. But Aaron's staff swallowed up their staffs.'

The cobra or *urae* was a symbol of the ruling power. This was the main symbol of the ruling pharaoh. Moses is showing Pharaoh that YHVH was the ruling power and he had the power to do whatever he wanted. Pharaoh must have thought far too highly of himself to allow what followed in Exodus 7 – 11 to happen.

Moses the prophet is the irritant in the side of Pharaoh, revealing Pharaoh's true nature, revealing YHVH's true authority and power.

Moses is the story of God's prophet speaking into the atrocity of the day, calling out the slave trade and leading people to freedom. If this were today, Moses would be seen as a liberator, someone who politically approaches an authority and speaks in such a way that brings revelation to the way the oppressor is behaving. Moses speaks into the political and social mess, pinpointing the systemic damnation of the oppressor's rule. He reveals the levels of oppression built into the system of the Egyptian empire. The systems of oppression that stem from fake-god worship; gods who ask for money, gifts, attention but are, in fact, nothing but creations of the Egyptians.

It was the gods that Pharaoh wanted to prove himself over; he wanted to prove he was the true authority, that he was the overarching god. It was his overblown view of himself that made him think he could turn God's people into forced labour.

Moses reveals Pharaoh's oppressive regime and is God's voice to the evil tyrant. Moses then sees the amazing sight of God's people finally being liberated into a land he is providing for them to live in, in freedom.

Preachers and prophets

Unbelief isn't a problem for God. Weakness isn't a problem for God. But unwillingness is a problem for him. God called Moses to speak the truth to Pharaoh, and he asks us to do the same to our leadership, locally and nation-ally.

We have mistaken Jesus for a preacher when in fact he was a politician, a prophet to the empire of his time. The resurrection community has become a silent preacher and needs to become a vocal politician, a prophet to the empire of our time. We need to re-find our identity not just as a resurrection community, but also as a community of prophets speaking clearly into the empires that are being built around us every day.

Thinking deeper

- In Genesis 1 we are called to dress and bless God's creation. How have you seen your relationship with creation previously? Has it changed now and, if so, how?
- What could you be doing to dress and bless creation each day?
- Have you seen the village, town or city where you live as God's arena before? Is your church involved in the local area? Are you involved in the local area?
- What could you be doing that might help the resurrection community be more in touch with local people, sports, schools, workplaces or governments?
- If we are called to be prophets and called to speak God's agenda for the poor, the oppressed and the abandoned, who is it that you need to speak out for, specifically?
- Maybe start thinking small. Is it the boss who needs to stock Fairtrade in the work café, is it the manager who needs to understand that their sexism isn't on, is it the racist cabbie that lives next door? Or could it be something bigger like the local government which needs to speak more clearly on people trafficking?
- Do you know what is going on in your area with regard to politics? Do you know who your local MP is?

Epilogue 9.

The Landing

I see breath in its lungs

I see a church around me that looks like a valley of dead dry bones, but there is hope because I see movement, the bones are stirring. Where before there was the smell of death, I now smell the aroma of life. There are tendons and muscles forming and growing, and bones are having a new Spirit breathed into them.

I see a church that is rising up.

Death to life.

A church being resurrected by a movement of people dreaming new dreams.

A church with a new heart and desire to see its land changed.

Changed not due to political power, not because of money or military force, but a church changing the nations because it is having love breathed into it, a church having muscles with love as its blood; a church that is   rising to build a better world in the name of Jesus, the homeless revolutionary from Nazareth. A church whose primary weapon is generosity, love, a willingness to listen before speaking. A church that is willing to hear the world's story before it gives another better story. A church which doesn't want to rip shreds off people, but see the best in them, and affirms it in the name of Jesus.

And when he puts his breath in those dead bones, people will look and know that he is God (Ezek. 37:5,6) and that his church, his ekklesia is alive and bearing fruit.

The Iranian Muslim refugee

Mr Sortie is an Iranian Muslim refugee who for some time has been hanging around my friend's church. Over a few weeks, my friend Mike started to build up a good friendship with him. Helping find Mr Sortie some accommodation near the church,

Mike has been able to spend lots of time hanging out, eating, chatting and hanging curtains. One night before Mike left to go home, Mr Sortie blurted out, 'You need to earn my friendship. I like spending time with you, but to be my friend you need to prove yourself as a friend, and so does your Jesus.' Mike turned to Mr Sortie and said, 'You don't have to earn my friendship, and neither do you have to earn Jesus.'

Mr Sortie has been blown away by this resurrection community's generosity. Furthermore, he has been blown away by Mike's friendship, and even more by Jesus'.

I have heard it said that Christians need to stop taking themselves too seriously. I believe this to be so wrong. I think Christians don't take themselves seriously enough. They don't take the call to be Jesus' hands and feet seriously enough. They behave like it's an optional extra, but it isn't; we are Jesus' way of breaking into this world.

Practising resurrection means we need the confidence that our God will come through. We need confidence that he can make something beautiful from our own selfishness, greed and desire. It's when we practise the reverence of every life that we start to see all the little resurrections budding around us. It is in our reverence for life that we see death, but we also see in the continued progress of creation new life emerging.

In the face of destruction

We need to practise resurrection in the face of a world that keeps causing destruction, often doing so at such a rapid rate.

Every time we bring new hope to a desperate situation, when we set people free from their own lies, when we choose to forgive, when we give back someone's dignity and welcome them back into the family, when we choose to listen and not to speak, when we listen and then affirm them and their life . . .

Whenever we bring joy to the joyless, when we shatter their despair, whenever we speak the truth and stand up for those on the underside, when we allow the past into God's mercy and we leave the future in God's hands, and we choose to live in the present moment seeing his work right here, right now . . .

When we encourage ourselves to make connections and allow the dividing wall of hostility to come crashing down, when we welcome guests and their alien ideas with grace, when we practise hospitality and give full rein to our imaginations, when we creatively look for a third option and seek to find other peaceful alternatives . . .

When we choose to see the beauty in everyone and look for God's likeness, when we choose to feed the hungry and clothe the orphan, when we affirm that all things can be made new and live knowing that God has made everything clean . . .

When we open our souls to the pain of the world, allow compassion to flood our hearts and acknowledge that 'love wins', when our little acts of kindness bring some fun into the world and we encourage another's sense of wonder, when we believe we are standing on holy ground and presume we have some part to play, when we are willing to work with others, allowing unity to bond us in trying to make the world a more just place . . .

Whenever we confront injustice and challenge the oppression, it is then that we join with Jesus in bringing people back to life.

We bring people back from the dead.

We move death to life.

Broken and poured out

I was chatting to a young guy at my church called Alex who had been out shopping for a new pair of jeans. He had spent his last few quid on a new pair of last season designer jeans, which were really good quality – and, many of us would argue, a much-needed investment for a student on little money. As he'd walked home from his shopping spree, he'd bumped into a man hanging out by the station. The guy had visited our church a few times and Alex had chatted to him on a couple of occasions. The guy was sleeping rough, and had been for a few months. The resurrection community had been working to find him a bed, but often he had found life simpler on the streets.

After a short chat, Alex had realized that the guy had a huge rip in his jeans and that he was about the same size as him. Alex had asked about clothes and it seemed that he had a change of tops but only the jeans he was wearing.

Reaching into the bag, Alex had pulled out his new jeans and given them to the homeless kid. The jeans were bought with Alex's last few quid, and now the jeans were going to hang on the homeless kid.

I was in Maseno, Africa, and the day I was due to leave I met a young man of around 19 who was walking around barefoot. His English wasn't great and my Swahili even worse. I understood that he was a farmer and that he didn't own his own shoes. Being only a short distance from the compound where I was staying, I slipped off my sandals and handed them to him. The good news was that they fitted, and I was very pleased to see him walking alongside me wearing my shoes. I hadn't realized how painful it was to walk barefoot. We walked side by side for some time until we got back to the compound.

For a moment I identified with his pain as I chose to walk barefoot.

He walked away walking in my world, as I now walked in his.

Serious resurrection

Practising resurrection is about taking Jesus' resurrection seriously, seeing ourselves as a part of the response to the world's *chatta't*. It's about praying for the poor but it's about giving away our own jeans. It's about walking away without something because we're willing to die to our own needs for the needs of others.

Taking off our own shoes, walking away shoeless, taking their place, taking their suffering.

In Alex's story, I see someone taking this movement seriously. I see this resurrection all around me each day as friends and resurrection family share their stories of dying to self to give life to others. Their stories give me hope.

Back in my teens, I went to Art College over the road from one of Leeds' small gig venues. This particular night a fresh-from-Take-That Robbie Williams was playing the venue and was stood outside having a smoke. I caught a glimpse of him putting out his cigarette and walking back inside. The window I saw him through was right next to my desk and I was desperate to catch a glimpse of him again. I was so interested to see him that I sat waiting and watching from my chair.

A number of lecturers came by to see why I wasn't doing what I should have been doing. They were less than impressed with my level of work that day. Sometimes when looking away I'd see something move outside from the corner of my eye and quickly look, only to see an old woman walking with her shopping trolley.

A number of years later, friends and I saw a guy camping with his family hit by lightning on a cliff top. He didn't die but did need to go to hospital. Whenever I went back to the campsite, I couldn't help but hope that I would see another weird event like this again.

Have you ever sat waiting to catch a glimpse of something, hoping to see the freak event or the pop star again?

The witnesses of Jesus' ascension were looking intently up to the sky in the hope of seeing Jesus flying around (Acts 1:10).

They wanted one last glimpse of Jesus. Do we blame them? Seeing Jesus ascending up into the sky must have been unbelievable! It must have been one of those 'Did I really see that happen?' events. Pre-Superman flight!

Suddenly two men dressed in white (a strange sight as people didn't have washing detergent to keep their clothes clean in those days) appeared by them. These witnesses were advised to stop looking to the sky; they had to start to look to the culture around them for their next steps, to see what needed to be done. What does it mean to live in such a way that brings the resurrection in everyday life?

The couple went to fetch their credit card.
The student handed him his jeans.
She was the first person to enter his flat in fifteen years.
She baptized her in the bath.
He drove to find medicine.
He made and served soup each day with no thanks.
She took her to Paris.
They served tea and coffee with cooked breakfast in the rain.
He hung some curtains for him.
He was invited into the family to pray for the Muslim boy . . .
And he got the coach to London to visit the embassy.

Always at work

Resurrection is all around us. It's at work because the Father is always at work. We are invited into a community that breathes life into the dead. A community existing for its non-members.

This kind of movement has captivated my heart, it moves me forward, it propels me to love and it has caused me to re-find my love for Jesus' ekklesia. Re-find my love for Jesus' church.

It causes me to take off my sandals and walk away barefoot because I have a part to play in the resurrection of the world.

Is that the kind of church you want to be a part of? It certainly is for me.

Practising Resurrection

What have we learnt?

- Resurrection changes everything.
- We need to live generously.
- And die generously.
- We need to see others as brothers and sisters.
- Jesus practised the awe of every life and so should we.
- We, too, can encourage a common and open life among those around us.
- Share economic resources with the needy brothers and sisters around us.
- Create peace wherever we can.
- Speak new, positive, life-giving words over people.
- Believe in scandalous grace.
- Give as much as we can away.
- Believe in the super and natural.
- Have a house of hospitality.
- Learn to hang curtains.
- We can be the answer to our prayers.
- Live eternally today.
- It's better to steer towards love than hate.
- Pull people in.
- Become a willing prophet.
- We should take out our credit card once in a while and accompany someone else shopping.

Further Reading

Resurrection

Peter Schmiechen, *Saving Power: Theories of Atonement and Forms of Church* (Grand Rapids: Eerdmans, 2005).

N.T. Wright, *The Resurrection of the Son of God* (London: SPCK, 2003).

N.T. Wright, *Jesus and the Victory of God* (London: SPCK, 1996).

History and Judaism:

Marcus J. Borg and John Dominic Crossan, *The Last Week* (London: SPCK, 2008).

Bruce Chilton and Jacob Neusner, *Judaism in the New Testament: Practices and Beliefs* (New York: Routledge, 1995).

David Flusser, *The Sage from Galilee: Rediscovering Jesus' Genius* (Grand Rapids, Michigan: Magnes Press, 1997).

Rabbi Neil Gillman, *The Jewish Approach to God* (Woodstock, Vermont: Jewish Lights Publishing, 2003).

Flavius Josephus, *The Complete Works of Josephus* (Nashville: Thomas Nelson Publishers, 1998).

Rabbi Lawrence Kushner, *Jewish Spirituality: A Brief Introduction for Christians* (Woodstock, Vermont: Jewish Lights Publishing, 2001).

Stephen Wylen, *The Jews in the Time of Jesus: An Introduction* (New York: Paulist Press, 1995).

Brad Young, *Meet the Rabbis* (Massachusetts: Henderson Publishers, 2007).

Brad Young, *The Parables* (Massachusetts: Henderson Publishers, 2008).

Brad Young, *Jesus the Jewish Theologian* (Massachusetts: Henderson Publishers, 1995).

History and politics

John Crossan, *God and Empire: Jesus Against Rome, Then and Now* (New York: Harper Collins, 2007).

Tod Lindberg, *The Political Teachings of Jesus* (New York: Harper Collins, 2007).

Alan Storkey, *Jesus and Politics: Confronting the Powers* (Grand Rapids: Baker Academic, 2005).

Walter Wink, *The Powers that Be* (New York: Random House, 1998).

N.T. Wright, *Evil and the Justice of God* (London: SPCK, 2006).

John Yoder, *The Politics of Jesus* (Grand Rapids: Eerdmans Publishing, 1972).

Other good reads

Dave Bookless, *Planetwise* (Nottingham: IVP, 2008).

Steve Chalke and Anthony Watkis, *Intelligent Church* (Grand Rapids: Zondervan, 2006).

Shane Claibourne, *The Irresistible Revolution* (Grand Rap-ids: Zondervan, 2006).

Shane Claibourne and Chris Haw, *Jesus for President* (Grand Rapids: Zondervan, 2008).

Oliver James, *Affluenza* (London: Vermilion, 2007).

Mark Kurlansky, *Nonviolence* (London: Jonathan Cape Publishing, 2006).

Oscar Romer, *The Violence of Love* (New York: Orbis Books, 2004).

Andre Trocme, *Jesus and the Nonviolent Revolution* (New York: Orbis Books, 2003).

N.T. Wright, *For All God's Worth: True Worship and the Calling of the Church* (Grand Rapids: Eerdmans Pub-lishing, 1997).

For those wanting to get into the Bible text and culture

Gilbert Beers, *Journey Through The Bible* (London: Monarch, 1981).

John Bowker, *The Complete Bible Handbook* (London: DK, 1998).

The Encyclopedia of World Myths (London: Anness Publishing, 2008).

Bruce Feiler, *Walking Through the Bible* (New York: Morrow, 2005).

The Jewish Study Bible (New York: Oxford University Press, 2004).

The Lion Encyclopaedia of the Bible (London: Lion Hudson, 2001).

James Michener, *The Source: A Novel* (New York: Random House, 2002).

Nick Page, *The Bible Book* (London: Harper Collins, 2002).

Miriam Vamosh, *Daily Life at the Time of Jesus* (Israel: Palphot, 2007).